Whispers of Better Things

Duncan Mackay is a former winner of the Henry Ford European Conservation Award for Heritage and former editor of the Twyford and Ruscombe Local History Society magazine. He has worked as Director of the South East region of the Countryside Agency; Environmental Manager for Berkshire County Council; and Deputy Secretary of the Commons, Open Spaces and Footpaths Preservation Society. He has written six books and contributed to others including *England in Particular* and *Food for Free* (2012 edition).

By the same author

The Secret Thames (Ebury Press, 1992)
Apples, Berkshire, Cider (Two Rivers Press (1996)
Eat Wild (Two Rivers Press, 2010)
Bizarre Berkshire (Two Rivers Press, 2012)
Reading: The Place of the People of the Red One (Two Rivers Press, 2016)

Also published by Two Rivers Press

Picture Palace to Penny Plunge: Reading's Cinemas by David Cliffe
The Shady Side of Town: Reading's Trees by Adrian Lawson and Geoff Sawers
A Wild Plant Year by Christina Hart-Davies
The Veiled Vale by Mike White
Before and After by Edith Morley, edited by Barbara Morris
Silchester by Jenny Halstead & Michael Fulford
The Writing on the Wall by Peter Kruschwitz
Caught on Camera by Terry Allsop
Allen W. Seaby by Martin Andrews & Robert Gillmor
Reading Detectives by Kerry Renshaw
Fox Talbot & the Reading Establishment by Martin Andrews
All Change at Reading by Adam Sowan
An Artist's Year in the Harris Garden by Jenny Halstead
Caversham Court Gardens by Friends of Caversham Court Gardens
Believing in Reading by Adam Sowan
Bikes, Balls & Biscuitmen by Tim Crooks & Reading Museum
The Reading Quiz Book by Adam Sowan
Broad Street Chapel & the Origins of Dissent in Reading by Geoff Sawers
Reading: A Horse-Racing Town by Nigel Sutcliffe
Down by the River by Gillian Clark
A Much-maligned Town by Adam Sowan
The Holy Brook by Adam Sowan
A Thames Bestiary by Peter Hay and Geoff Sawers
Abattoirs Road to Zinzan Street by Adam Sowan

Whispers of Better Things

Green Belts to National Trust
How the Hill family changed our world

Duncan Mackay

TWO
RIVERS
PRESS

First published in the UK in 2017 by Two Rivers Press
7 Denmark Road, Reading RG1 5PA
www.tworiverspress.com

ISBN 978-1-909747-33-3

1 2 3 4 5 6 7 8 9

Two Rivers Press is represented in the UK by Inpress Ltd and distributed by NBNi.

Cover design and illustration by Nadja Guggi
Text design by Nadja Guggi and typeset in Parisine

Printed and bound in Great Britain by Imprint Digital, Exeter

To Len Clark CBE

Len and I started working for the Commons, Open Spaces and Footpaths Preservation Society around the same time in 1978. We quickly became firm friends and allies in the struggle to ensure that as much remnant common land as possible was legally recorded after the Commons Registration Act 1965 came into force, but that was only one of his interests.

Len seemed to know just about everything about everyone involved in what is now called the 'conservation movement' and offered valuable lessons in the art of how to achieve things. His techniques of persuasion were like a Swiss Army knife, if one bit didn't work then he would reveal another, possibly sharper, tool. In this way he amiably nobbled Countryside Commissioners, Directors of the National Trust, Youth Hostels Association, National Parks, Wildlife Trusts, MPs and members of the House of Lords by simply applying and reapplying his persistently made, cogently argued case for action. He seemed to have a sixth sense for those who could be most effectively persuaded (and a knack of making most electronic machinery dysfunction; he had to be kept away from photocopiers, particularly). To enable this lobbying to take place Len had an ageing Honda 90 scooter, a helmet, copious layers of flapping waterproofs and a little brown rucksack, which carried him to the remotest parts of England and Wales. On wet winter days, Len's arrival into a warm office would generate small clouds as various articles of outdoor weather-proofing would be dried on hot radiators and soggy papers restored to rigidity. Nothing fazed Len. He would drop little *bons mots* into conversation, 'Just got the Trust to acquire 16,000 acres of Welsh common', or 'Just met a terrific girl at the Council for National Parks', or 'Just off to see the Director-General about the South Downs'. When questioned about why he was motor biking 200 miles in the rain to some faraway place he would casually reply, with a twinkle, 'Just keeping an eye on things'.

Len, now 101, is one of the warmest, wittiest, generously nicest people I have ever met and his long life is a constant inspiration to do better things.

Duncan Mackay, September 2017

Acknowledgements

The idea for this book began nearly forty years ago when I started reading about the inspiring work of Sir Robert Hunter, Octavia Hill and other leaders of the 'open space movement'. This was augmented by Len Clark's knowledge of where these early activities had led, particularly in relation to the National Trust and the Youth Hostels Association. At times, when trying to save commons, I found myself asking the rhetorical question, 'what would Octavia or Robert do?' Around this time (the late 1970s) I also first met Fiona Reynolds at the Council for National Parks. The 'environmental movement', of which we were all a part, was attempting to change things for the better in the spirit of the age and we were heavily involved in countryside legislation and lobbying. Fiona was its rising star and reached the perihelion of careers in the environmental sector when she was deservedly appointed as Director-General of the National Trust and made a Dame. I am very grateful to Fiona for sparing the time, despite her demanding new role as Master of Emmanuel College, Cambridge, to write the foreword for 'Whispers'.

A number of people have generously given their time to make these whispers louder. At the National Trust Dame Helen Ghosh, the ever-helpful Jon Powlesland and the ever-active Ellie Robinson helped me to understand its developing role assisting local authorities to manage their urban parks. At Historic England, Jennifer White and colleagues provided some of the references associated with Octavia Hill's female relationships. The recent research work to assess my idea for 'new commons' was led by Professor Chris Rodgers of the University of Newcastle-upon-Tyne and supported by writer and Cambridge University academic Robert Macfarlane as well as Euan Hall, CEO of the Land Trust. Without their interest it would not have been possible to test the concept.

In Oregon, travel writer Ana Murmann offered me an American perspective on the first draft and I am very grateful to the Lindgren family for the peace of their Finnish lakeside summerhouse (and sauna!) that helped me edit. Closer to home, a chance meeting at the Circus Sauce dinner tent at Giffords Circus in Daylesford introduced me to the natural healing powers of Judy from Northleach. Within ten minutes she had straightened two of my Dupuytren's contracted fingers enabling me to type without pain. Six months later they are still straight, so huge thanks Judy. At home, my dear wife Viv has suffered piles of books cluttering the dinner table and my long absences at the computer with loving grace and sweetness.

The Two Rivers Press editorial team of Sally Mortimore, Adam Sowan, Barbara Morris and Theresa Millar, has been enthusiastic and constructively critical in the pursuit of print perfection, as always, and masterful at spotting the unpredictable results of predictive text. Nadja Guggi came up with the idea for the cover illustration and has created another superbly designed book. Thanks to Karen Mosman for securing copyright permissions. Thanks too for the enduring work of previous writers and researchers in all formats and fashions, particularly Octavia Hill's biographer, Gillian Darley.

Daniel Raven-Ellison is a self-styled 'guerrilla geographer' and a determined innovator in the style of the Hills. He, almost single-handedly, set out the case for Greater London to be the world's first 'National Park City'. My thanks to Dan for his fulsome comments and continuing interest. Dr Victoria Edwards jointly presented a paper on new commons with me in Bologna and is now the CEO of the Ernest Cook Trust. Her opinions are always erudite and sharp and I'm really pleased by her support.

Illustrations

The pictures of Octavia and James Hill on pp. xii and 15 respectively are taken from https://commons.wikimedia.org/wiki/ and were originally published in *Life of Octavia Hill as told in her letters by Hill, Octavia, 1838–1912*; Maurice, C. Edmund (Charles Edmund), ed. Macmillan and Co, Limited, London; 1913.

The picture of Arthur Hill on p. 24 is from a document owned by the Berkshire Record Office (D/EX1638/71) and reproduced with their permission and our gratitude for their friendly service.
© Berkshire Record Office.

The photograph of the Red Cross Cottages on p. 47 was taken in 2017 by Duncan Mackay, the author. © Duncan Mackay.

The cartoon on p. 50, London going out of Town, was designed, etched & published by George Cruikshank on 1 November 1829. Permission to reproduce it here has kindly been granted by its owners:
© The Trustees of the British Museum.

The Map of green spaces on p. 55 was taken from https://ntpressoffice.wordpress.com/tag/more-air-for-london and we can't find the original owners despite conscientious searching. Any information that would help us solve this mystery would be much appreciated by the publisher.

Quotations

The quotes set in bold throughout the book are from various sources which are asterisked in the further reading section on p. 100.

Foreword

There is every reason to regard Octavia Hill as one of history's most inspirational figures. Housing and green spaces campaigner, a founder of the National Trust and a pioneering woman at a time when women's voices were too rarely heard: she has long been a heroine of mine.

But to many, her large family, close friends and the people with whom she worked and on whom she leaned have remained somewhat shadowy figures, even though they had a huge influence on Octavia's hard working life. Now Duncan Mackay has set out to put that right. In this book he charts the people who shaped Octavia's early life and ideas, worked with her during her long years as a pioneer of a new model for social housing and advocate for green spaces, and stayed with her through her long life.

I'm particularly moved by the stories of Octavia's sisters. Being one of five girls myself I'm intrigued by the dynamics of large families, and especially the relationships between sisters. Miranda Hill, especially, deserves more attention and hopefully this book will encourage more people to take an interest in her.

Above all Duncan captures the spirits, thinkers and intellects who surrounded Octavia, helping explain how her passion for beauty, and thus the foundation for a lifetime's achievement, emerged.

Dame Fiona Reynolds
Master, Emmanuel College
Former Director-General, National Trust

Contents

Octavia Hill's portrait from 1882 as a youthful 43-year-old.

'We all need space; unless we have it,
we cannot reach that sense of quiet
in which whispers of better things
come to us gently.'

—Octavia Hill, 1888

Introduction

This book narrates the truly astonishing achievements of the Victorian-era Hill family, the people who inspired them and those who were inspired by them. Chief amongst their achievements was the co-creation of the National Trust via the Society for the Diffusion of Beauty, a body that virtually nobody knows of today. The social origin of the threads that formed the weft and warp of the fabric of this mighty institution and other bodies was a reaction by Christian, middle-class people to the widespread suffering of the urbanised working classes. This might be considered as 'do-goodery' or cynically smoothing your own path to the afterlife with kind deeds, but it was clearly much more than that in terms of its intent and impact. The Hill family were startlingly different people. This difference was marked by a curiously benevolent blending of medical welfare knowledge, Christian Socialism bound together with Pestalozzian educational principles, Owenite radicalism and strong female relationships. Haunting it all was the deep dread of falling into debt and being cast amongst the destitute in the workhouse, as the 'undeserving' poor, the 'living dead' of the Victorian Industrial Revolution. This was a matter of critical, middle-class importance, as Charles Dickens discovered, and produced family members that, usually, supported each other in the perilous game of economic snakes and ladders. They provided 'cover' whenever unpredictable disasters beset them, even if, as in the Hill family, there were, through early death and mental illness, children by three different mothers and one latterly absent father.

In that era of 'devil take the hindmost' *laissez-faire* economics, pleas for the poor, the provision of decent housing, urban and urban fringe public open spaces, places for children to play, access to greenery, sunlight, clean air, natural beauty and a 'right to air and exercise' to lead healthier lives, were initiated by the redoubtable Hills. Some of this pleading was stimulated by their forebears' concerns for better public health, social justice, universal education and sanitation. There was, eventually, a huge response then and, arguably, because of subsequent population expansion, there is an even greater need for a bigger response now. It is a continuously evolving story. We all need space.

> 'We all need space; unless we have it, we cannot reach that sense of quiet in which whispers of better things come to us gently.'
> —Octavia Hill, 1888

The Hills were also leaders of smoke abatement but in just over a century of 'progress' we have swapped smoggy coal-smoke pollution for deathly diesel fumes; Victorian malnutrition and hunger for a sugar-led obesity epidemic; and the deadly diseases of hard labour for the killer diseases of inactivity. *Plus ça change, plus c'est la même chose* (the more it changes, the more it's the same thing).

The battle for the preservation of the greenery of the Green Belt today is something that the Hills would recognise, mainly because they invented the term 'Green Belt'. The 'whispers of better things' envisaged by the Hills' principal spokesperson for land to be shared amongst the landless for the health, happiness and better wellbeing of the many is still a tiny voice. Maybe it is something that requires our urgent amplification before the 'sense of quiet' is drowned out by the ugly din of rampant development. We all need space but in the 1873 Parliamentary survey it was found that 100 per cent of the land in England was owned by just 4.5 per cent of the population; now 70 per cent is owned by just 0.6 per cent of the population. *Plus ça change …*

Whispers of Better Things is a journey through times and spaces. The Hill family was, briefly, nucleated in Wisbech, a small Cambridge-shire town in the flat Fenland countryside, but only half of its origins lie there. Although some remained, the others did not stay there long, nor indeed, together – some moving on first to Essex then Hampstead, Gloucester, Leeds and finally back to London's outskirts Finchley and London town itself. The others departed to Worksop, Boston and Reading. The impacts of this family and its network of contacts on Victorian society were profound and the long-term legacy of their and their associates' achievements is still being enjoyed today by tens of millions of people. Some people living today undoubtedly even owe their existence to the life-saving achievements of this cluster of individuals. So, who on earth were they, how did the events they brought about arise, and what exactly did they do? It is a complicated map but I have tried to simplify it whilst leaving enough signposts for those who might want to follow longer and more detailed routes.

This book is also a description of strong-willed women, women who overcame prejudice in the Victorian era of male domination, and indeed of women who preferred women to men and created their own universes including same-sex love and care in a sea of sometimes even riotous misogynous hostility. In an era when there was no word for lesbianism or bisexuality, the language became blurred and many female 'companions' seem to have existed in the literature of the time – perhaps as a proxy term, or perhaps not. When most women were merely chattels, unable to own property if married or to be themselves as professionals or intellectuals, and simply regarded as baby-production machines during the entirety of their fecundity, anyone who didn't marry stood out as odd. The benefits of this 'oddness' were clear and, as there was no energy-sapping drainage from being permanently pregnant or housebound with a dozen children, it was possible to energetically make the world a better place. As we will see, Miranda, Octavia and Florence Hill never married and surrounded themselves with fellow female workers or women who seem to have shared a similar attitude towards life. Their actions, and the enabling financial support of other, much wealthier, women, definitely made the world a better place. The National Trust website notes that:

'Hill's lack of interest in marriage and her passionate friendship with other women formed a life-path that was common among independent-minded Victorian women. In the early 1860s she had a friendship with Sophia Jex-Blake, who led the fight for women's entry to the medical profession. In May 1860 Jex-Blake confided to her diary that Hill "sunk her head on my lap silently, raised it in tears, and then such a kiss".'

In September 2016 Historic England (the government's advisory body) included Octavia Hill in its compilation of notable LGQBT female history-makers, based on evidence relating to her short relationship with Sophia Jex-Blake as a young woman.

The Hills were sandwiched between the impoverished working classes and the outrageously wealthy elites. Their story was a bourgeois tale of middle-class social placement emerging through a froth of religious and moral challenges raging between the established church, dissenters, Christian Socialists and others. Mix in ideas of obligation, duty, 'service to others' 'self-help', abstinence, plain living and inner reflection during an extreme period of capitalistic brutality, and it is easy to see how the countering efforts of social reform and suffrage found a niche. The bones of the body of this confusing epoch can be glimpsed from our position looking back but we can probably never understand all the moral, economic and religious complexities of those who lived through it. Historians have attributed gentrification tendencies to Octavia Hill's rigid rules of social housing care and other writers have accused Miranda Hill's Society for the Diffusion of Beauty (later renamed the Kyrle Society) of being aesthetic nonsense. However, these unashamedly middle-class individuals, whatever their faults, foibles and frailties, *did* something, rather than just pontificating about doing something, or even worse, promising one thing and doing the opposite. Other members of the Hill brood did things differently or more quietly but all had extended family connections that reinforced their collective endeavours.

Despite the Hills being driven and determined individuals who spotted opportunities and took their chances, there was never any certainty that their efforts would succeed. Some critical social links and connections might seem accidental, incidental or haphazard, but the totality of 'the work', as Octavia Hill called it, has created some of the social and environmental products and institutions that inform our modern lives. These items form a long list and make life more bearable than it might otherwise have been if the counter forces to this 'service to others' had achieved their ambitions of sustained selfishness and greed. The contributions of one of the maternal Hill grandfathers, Thomas Southwood Smith, include the development of public health and sanitation, stopping children working down mines and helping prevent orphans from being beaten to death in grim factories.

Narrating the struggle of a small number of people committed to the cause of creating beauty and goodness over ugliness and badness may stir a sense of homage. However, the Hills were never perfect people, but beings driven by strong desires for self-actualisation whilst suffering their own demons of doubt and despair. I hope this book allows some judgement that their instincts were right, that the products of their 'work' initiatives are still relevant to many people's lives today, and that it is a continuing story that begs our urgent attention and action. Miranda Hill, in particular perhaps, has been greatly overlooked by history but her key contribution was to supply the quiet emotional intelligence to seek and speak out for 'beauty' and to stir a pot that still gives intellectual nourishment today, particularly as urbanisation increases. Miranda did not create volumes of letters to fellow workers, grab the headlines or publish polemical papers every week like her younger sister, but her sprinkling of ideas was the fairy-dust from which much else sparkled. Arguably, it would be true to say that it was Miranda who lit the torch for 'natural beauty on the doorstep' that Octavia used to illuminate the path to the National Trust for Places of Historic Interest and Natural Beauty and led to modern protected countryside landscape designations such as Areas of Outstanding Natural Beauty. The task now is to return these initiatives for natural beauty to the cities, towns and urban fringes from whence they came, in ideas such as National Park Cities, currently being mooted for Greater London, utilising tools like natural capital evaluation.

Who, wherever they reside, does not want to live amongst beauty and open spaces, or enjoy a better quality of life's experience? Everything is learning and we can all learn to be better and do beautiful things. The Hills show how the seemingly impossible can be achieved by any of us.

The Hill family

Both nurture and nature are important elements in the Hill family story. This portion of *Whispers of Better Things* attempts to bring us closer to a deeper understanding of the inter-generational relations and relationships that brought the elements together. It is a mysterious alchemy that creates these family thought-forms and ideas that might emerge at any point as living creations like Tibetan *tulpa*.

An oft-repeated family yarn or an amusing inter-generational shaggy-dog story or simply the sense of 'in our family we have a saying' are items that can transfer through time like heirlooms. What seems remarkable, however, are the chance encounters, the puzzling crossroads of circumstance, of routes followed, or paths *not* taken, the matrix of people who know other people who just happened to be around when they were discussing 'that idea'. There is a seemingly metaphysical matrix of parts that came together to create something new, something that also changed our world today.

This section could be regarded as a quasi-forensic examination of the Hill story, a kind of family dissection of 'where did that idea come from?' No family story is ever complete, but these glimpses might offer a simple route back through time to begin the process of understanding a little more about high ideals, morals, motivations and the intellectual boundaries of the age, and those who operated at the edges of those borders. It starts with the grandparents.

The grandparents

THOMAS SOUTHWOOD SMITH, 1788–1861

Maternal grandfather Thomas was born in Somerset near Martock on the winter solstice 21 December 1788. He was encouraged into Calvinistic religious study at 14 by the award of a Baptist scholarship in Bristol. However, before he was 18 his doubts about Calvinism led him to consider other dissenting branches and he was tempted into Unitarianism by Rev. William Blake, the minister in Crewkerne. In a

Grandparents	Parents	Children

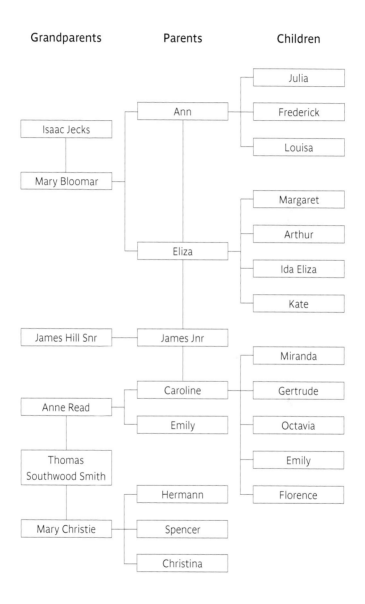

deeply religious Baptist household this unspeakable alternative view created an irreparable rift. During his time as a student he had been many times to the house of Mr Read, a Baptist pottery manufacturer and supporter of the College. He had a daughter called Anne who became attracted to Thomas. They probably married (without the blessing of his parents but supported by his in-laws) in or before 1808. By 1809 Anne had given birth to Caroline and a year later to Emily (1810–1872). Their happiness as young parents was short-lived as Anne died in 1812.

Here, at this dramatic turning point in his life at the age of just 23, grieving for his dead wife, divorced from his parents and family by religious dogma, cut off from his career and with two toddlers under three to support, the decision of what to do next must have been wracking. Training to become a doctor in Edinburgh seems an odd choice under the circumstances, but leaving the girls in the care of their kindly grandparents, Thomas went to Scotland. However, after enrolling at the University of Edinburgh in 1813 and spending a lonely year at his studies, the agony of separation between father and daughters sent Thomas back to Bristol to collect Caroline, who although only four, took the storm-tossed sea route back to Edinburgh to live with her father and be educated at home. Emily remained in Bristol and was raised there before departing later for Italy.

Thomas and Caroline both learned some important lessons from these dramatic and traumatic events. These, in turn, later play a strong role in the creation of the family legend. Clearly there is evidence of intelligence, determination, fearlessness to overcome adversity, finding a better pathway (whether religious or otherwise), practicality and a drive for education (whether for soul, spirit or body). Some of these traits will appear later in a variety of forms.

After receiving his medical degree Thomas left Edinburgh with Caroline and moved first to Yeovil in 1816. Thomas lavished great love and attention on Caroline's upbringing and had home-schooled her in between his medical studies and preaching as a Unitarian; the lifelong bond between them was extraordinarily strong as a result of these shared experiences. In Yeovil he married Mary Christie, the daughter of John Christie from Hackney, who bore him a son, Hermann, in 1819 (died 1897) before the family moved to London in 1820. Thomas worked at the London Fever Hospital as well as settling into medical premises in Trinity Square at Tower Hill with his new wife and baby and Caroline. Amidst outbreaks of fevers and agues, Thomas began to realise that the process of 'sanitation' as it was then called – the isolation and forcible containment or quarantine (sometimes of whole cities, like Naples) – was not curing the source of the problem. While working with typhus patients in the East End slums of Whitechapel close to the hospital, Thomas started to postulate, in articles in the *Westminster Review*, that bad hygiene, bad water and even worse, bad human waste disposal, were the key causative factors, not mysterious 'miasmas'. The word 'sanitation' began to change its meaning from this point onwards and led to everything that the modern era knows as toilets, drains and wash basins or 'sanitary ware'.

Sometime in the 1820s or early 1830s (possibly related to the banking crises that affected James Hill in 1825, see p. 14) financial troubles resulted in the separation of Thomas from his wife Mary, who took her children, now including Spencer and Christina (later to die in childhood), abroad. Mary did not return until 1854 and died at The Pines in Weybridge in 1858. Caroline and sister Emily were now teaching elsewhere so Thomas moved as a single man into cheaper premises in 36 New Broad Street. More articles on public health, education and, in 1825, 'body snatching' appeared in the radical *Westminster Review*. His article 'The Use of the Dead to the Living' brought to public attention the lack of bodies for dissection in the medical schools and why the (legalised) supply of executed criminals was not keeping up with demand. Hence the gruesome trade of stealing dead bodies from graveyards. In 1828 the trial of 'resurrection men' Burke and Hare brought Thomas's paper to the attention of Parliament. His solution was to legalise the use, for medical science, of the more numerous unclaimed bodies of those who died in workhouses and hospitals (the proposal that later became known as 'donating your body to science'). The philosopher **Jeremy Bentham** voluntarily led the way.

In 1830 Dr Thomas Southwood Smith published his book *Treatise on Fever,* which revolutionised the way in which the causes (poverty and bad living conditions) of these pestilences were viewed. He stated:

> 'These poor people are victims that are sacrificed. The effect is the same as if twenty or thirty thousand of them were annually taken away from their homes and put to death.'

As part of the prevention of fevers 'an abundance of fresh air and scrupulous cleanliness' were given the highest importance. He even drew a six-mile radial circle on a map of the East End and visited every part of it to assess which areas suffered the most fevers (a tactic copied by Octavia Hill in the 1880s in the cause of open space deficiencies). He cited an instance in the Whitechapel Workhouse where young children never left a single small room for 'air or exercise'. The idea that poor public health was directly linked to poverty would also feature in his granddaughter's era, albeit modified in the cause of increasing better health through open-air recreation. The roots of the Open Space Movement start here.

Further commissions were to follow Thomas's growing fame and enabled him, in the *Royal Commission on Factories* (which led to the Factories Act 1833), to report on the deplorable conditions in workplaces where poor orphans from London workhouses and local children were often beaten, crippled, or almost worked to death in wool, cotton and silk mills. A minimum age of eight and maximum hours of work were thereafter imposed as well as compulsory part-time schooling. His 1834 book *The Philosophy of Health* began to set out the ideas that informed some of the thinking behind the later National Health Service and throughout the 1830s he continued to strive for the sanitary revolution and the introduction of public sewers and drainage systems. In 1840 the *Children's Employment Commission*, in an effort to prevent boys under ten and girls and women working in mines (often semi-naked, in deplorable conditions of foul air and complete darkness), sought his help as a Commissioner.

'Life is not long enough for us to reconsider our decisions.'

In 1840 Thomas agreed to adopt his granddaughter Gertrude (see p. 17). She came to reside with him and the artistic Gillies sisters in Kentish Town, one of whom, Margaret, was then living with Thomas and who would later inspire Octavia Hill's inner artist.

Thomas Southwood Smith helped create the Health of Towns Association and 'model dwellings', a movement to build blocks of sanitary and well-ventilated homes for the working classes. He also invented the 'nursing home' to embody all the principles of fresh air, natural surroundings, peace and quiet, good food and sanitary cleanliness that he believed aided patient recovery. The first of his 'sanatoriums' was created at Devonshire House in Regent's Park in 1842 and brought him to the attention of **Charles Dickens**, then at the height of his popularity and who lived opposite. Dickens asked him to help him do further research on conditions in Cornish mines, and it is believed that the doctor in *Bleak House* is based upon Thomas.

In 1846 grandfather, granddaughter and the Gillies sisters moved from Kentish Town to 'Hillside' in Fitzroy Court, Highgate, where they stayed until 1854. Here Gertrude lived the country lifestyle amidst hayfields, wildflower meadows, cows, chickens, goats and a pony called Ariel. Her sisters, particularly Miranda and Octavia, came to visit first from Finchley and later Russell Place down the hill in the smoky slums of Marylebone. This house and its closeness to rural simplicity became the 'open space ideal' of accessible natural beauty that the Hill sisters captured in their minds when campaigning. It was a short walk away from Swiss Cottage Common. Here, too, influential friends such as **Hans Christian Andersen**, Professor Richard Owen, William and Mary Howitt and **Robert Browning** visited.

Leigh Hunt called Thomas 'the Physician to Mankind' although the sanitation lawyer Edwin Chadwick is more fêted. After further Commissions and legislative battles to create the Public Health Act

1848 and lead its implementation, Thomas retired to The Pines, St George's Hill, Weybridge, in 1854, where he spent most of the rest of his life. He died, after catching a chill on a bridge over the Arno in Florence, Italy, while visiting his daughter Emily, and was buried there in December 1861. His last words were:

'Draw up the blind and let me see the stars; for I still love the beauty.'

JAMES HILL SNR (paternal grandfather) set up corn merchant businesses in Peterborough and Wisbech linked by the navigable River Nene in 1794. This generated wealth and created a small private bank that James Hill (father) and his brother Thomas inherited along with the other enterprises. A predecessor, James Hill (great-grandfather), had been born in Uppingham in the tiny county of Rutland in 1748; one of his ancestors, Sir Robert Hill a minor official to Henry IV, hailed from Shilstone near Modbury in Devon. The Hills had gradually wasted their manorial inheritance over the centuries, become landless and relocated to East Anglia, although still affluent.

ISAAC JECKS (maternal grandfather to the children of Ann and Eliza Jecks) was born 3 February 1756 in Wisbech and married **MARY BLOOMAR** (daughter of Newcombe Bloomar and Sarah Barrett, born 6 December 1759 in St Mary, Nottingham) at Newark on Trent. Isaac and Mary had eleven children who were baptised at the Unitarian Baptist Church in Wisbech. Mary died on 4 January 1851 at Framlington Pigot near Norwich at the age of 91. Isaac was similarly long-lived and died aged 85 in Chapel Field, St Giles, Norwich. In these late years they accepted the role of shared guardianship to their motherless grandchildren Margaret Hill, Ida Eliza Hill and Kate Hill.

Isaac owned houses on the riverside at 7 North Brink, Wisbech (1802) and West Walton in Norfolk (1806) and moved between businesses in drapery and grocery with a partner called Richard Dawbarn Banbury in Wisbech before later establishing a timber yard with his sons Charles and William.

'Few men have descended to the grave with a more spotless reputation or more deservedly respected. During eighty years Mr. Jecks has never known a day's illness and was walking about his home within an hour of his death. Lamented and respected by a numerous circle of friends, it may be truly said that strict integrity and universal benevolence marked his character.'

The parents

JAMES HILL JNR (father)

James was born in Modbury, Devon. He was three times married and twice widowed (sisters, **Ann Jecks** d. 1823 and **Eliza Jecks** d. 1832) and fathered the twelve Hill family children. He and his younger brother Thomas were rich, enterprising local businessmen with a strong Unitarian religious belief and social conscience. The main business of the brothers was the steamboat service between the towns of Peterborough and Wisbech, but interests also included their father's private country bank and corn merchant business. James Hill Jnr soon discovered that whilst banking proved to be successful during periods of corn-growing prosperity (such as the Napoleonic War) it was a highly risky business when external conditions changed. The 1825 banking crisis started to be noticed in April when the Bank of England (then a private bank) started pulling in its bank notes and loans. The market got twitchy as stock was sold by investors and then slid rapidly downwards. In the autumn of 1825 the Wentworth, Chaloner and Rishworth Bank in Wakefield, Yorkshire collapsed and the Hills' bank became one of the casualties in the national financial panic that followed, bankrupting both James and his father with a debt of £14,000.

James reopened the bank in Wisbech in the 1830s after paying off his creditors and also expanded his commercial concerns to include a timber merchant business. Tragedy struck again in 1832 when his second wife, Eliza, died (following the death of his first wife Ann in 1823). He now had six children and several businesses to manage, although his kindly in-laws were very close. He had almost superhuman levels of energy, a strongly reformist social conscience and was interested in many good things, including education. Even in his grieving he managed to find some articles written by a young woman on Pestalozzian education that closely matched his own ideas. He wrote to the editor of the *Monthly Repository* for the address of the author and went to Wimbledon with an offer to home-school his children. Later in 1832 Caroline Southwood Smith arrived in Wisbech to live at 8 South Brink as governess to the Hill

James Hill – a banker turned social reformer and Utopian.

children and, perhaps unsurprisingly, in 1835 she became engaged to be the third wife of James Hill and stepmother to his children.

James and Caroline married in London on 2 November 1835 at St Botolph's around the time that James's new father–in–law was achieving a growing reputation as a sanitation reformer and righter of wrongs. He also introduced James to **Robert Owen** from whom he heard firsthand about Owen's factory school in New Lanark. The Hills decided to open a school based on **Johann Heinrich Pestalozzi**'s theories and Owen's model so that the poor children of Wisbech could benefit from their combined energy and innovative schooling methods. In 1837 when the school opened, these infants were taught not only subjects but also

'the importance of truth, justice and mutual kindness and forbearance'.

More Hill children quickly followed and the world seemed to heading in a good direction. In 1836 James started a weekly Wisbech penny newspaper, *Star in the East,* to promote his new Owenite views. Then, in 1837, he attempted to start a colony at Wretton for the National Community Friendly Society but it failed when he insisted on directing its affairs. In 1838 he founded the United Advancement Society with the intention of buying land to live on and to counter the local Wisbech establishment. He managed to upset and inspire people in equal measure. As part of his local anti-corruption and establishment reform measures he fought against the harsh justice meted out for minor crimes (he once rode 50 miles overnight on horseback to Cambridge to secure a pardon for the last man to be condemned to death for sheep stealing) and founded a mechanics institute and a lending library. The school doubled up as a playhouse (it still is today) and over the door was a cleverly amended quote from William Wordsworth's *Rob Roy's Grave* poem to inspire the young students. It now echoes through time to the present and the title of this book. The 'whispers of better things' that his eighth daughter Octavia was to champion much later in her life in her emotionally intelligent appeals for a better world in the form of open spaces for the poor are possibly derived from the inspiring motto of this tiny school in Wisbech.

'Of old things all are over-old
Of good things none are good enough
We'll try if we can help to mould
A World of Better Stuff'

In 1840, shortly after Octavia was born, that much hoped-for better world began to crumble. Another banking crisis erupted and James again became bankrupt in a countrywide financial panic that also took down the Manea Fen Colony, an Owenite utopia led by **William Hodson**. This time there was no easy road back and all the Hills' assets had to be liquidated to pay the creditors as far as they could. James crashed into a deep depression but Caroline strove, with scrupulous accountancy, to keep business creditors in check and family responsibilities together. It soon became clear, however, that they would need to sell the family home and disperse the elder children to the care of the redoubtable Jecks, who took in the children of their deceased daughters Ann and Eliza.

With Caroline now pregnant again, Gertrude, their three-year-old, was sent to London to be adopted by her maternal grandfather (see p. 11) who also came to the rescue by renting a cottage in Loughton (Epping Forest) for the remnant family. James seemed to have rekindled some of his energy in Essex attempting to found a new Owenite colony before the family moved again to Hampstead, Gloucester and Leeds. In 1843 his final child was born in Leeds. With Owen himself in America, the Chartists in Leeds such as **Samuel Smiles** (the author of *Self-Help*), Feargus O'Connor, George Harney and the Owenites were falling out with each other. In 1845 James bought the publishing title of their main newsletter the *New Moral World* for £180. James changed the title to the *Commonweal* as a propaganda sheet for his latest idea, the National Land and Building Association, although only three editions were printed, all in 1845. It was subtitled as the *'development of a measure for advancing the political, the social, and the domestic conditions of the working classes'.* There is a curious crossover here to the later National Trust that has, as its main objects of care, land and buildings. Maybe the Hills later recalled James's ideas from family discussions. Perhaps the idea lodged with them, although its main aim was to buy agricultural land for industrial workers to become colonist agrarians. The Chartist Land Company took over the idea in 1847 as, by then, James had suffered another mental relapse, leading to isolation from his family. A product of this movement was Charterville in Minster Lovell, West Oxfordshire, where 78 cottages with smallholdings, a school and a meeting room were created in 1847–48. Owenite 'schools' and 'meeting rooms' were to become a motif of the later Hill family initiatives in social housing too. In 1858 James was again engaging with some of his daughters but too wretched to contemplate rejoining them. James died in Sydenham in 1872.

ANN JECKS (first wife of James Hill), born in Wisbech, Norfolk c. 1797, married in St Peter's Church, Wisbech 1818 and died 23 Nov 1823 aged 26. Mother of Julia, Frederick and Louisa.

ELIZA JECKS (second wife of James Hill), born 6 October 1802, sister of Ann, married James Hill on 31 May 1825 in Wisbech and died 28 Oct 1832 aged 30. This marriage was deemed illegal under the tables of Affinity in Ecclesiastical Law but James and Eliza didn't recognise the jurisdiction of the established church in these matters. Mother of Margaret, Arthur, Ida Eliza and Kate.

CAROLINE SOUTHWOOD SMITH (third wife of James Hill), born 21 March 1809 and died in 1902 aged 94. Mother of Miranda, Gertrude, Octavia, Emily and Florence.

From her own early, motherless, upbringing with her father in Bristol, Edinburgh and then in Yeovil, Caroline undoubtedly learned quiet self-reliance and order. These qualities suited her choice of work as a teacher when she moved to Wimbledon. Like her doctor father she realised that writing papers on subjects that were both important and interesting was a way to make a mark on the world. She was an adept writer and passionate about the teaching methods of the Swiss educator **Johan Heinrich Pestalozzi** and became the first ever Englishwoman to teach Pestalozzian schooling. She was also a faithful Unitarian.

In a brief whirlwind the energetic James Hill whisked her off to Wisbech. Here, as a live-in governess, her skills of social diplomacy within the home, and the ability to fit in to life with dissident James in Wisbech commerce and society as well as with the Jecks family would have been essential. Caroline seems to have carried all of this off with courteous aplomb and reputational stature, despite the fact that she was barely five feet tall.

The Wisbech school may have been a shared brainchild and it was obviously important to both of them to undertake this project. There seems little space between conception and making it happen. This is another important trait in understanding how the Hill family seems to have applied itself in later years in making many more 'impossible' things just 'happen'. All the experience of doing things right and doing the right thing would have been patiently drummed into the children from an early age. 'There's no such thing as can't', as the saying goes.

In 1840 the school was just beginning to become a firm feature of the Wisbech social scene (it was also a 'Hall of the People' in the evenings) when James suffered his second and most catastrophic bankruptcy. It must have been a soul-destroying feeling to lock the school door for the last time and bid goodbye to Wisbech and the solidity of a family home for the uncertainty of debt, penury, mental ill-health and a semi-nomadic life around the country in rented accommodation with unknowable economic prospects. There was no social or economic safety net other than Caroline's father's generosity.

Their arrival in the countryside village of Finchley, then some way beyond the built edge of London, after leaving their last port of call, industrial Leeds, was probably as much a relief to Caroline as it was to her remaining straggling brood of children. Despite the absence of a husband's fatherly hand, Caroline seems to have controlled the situation. The girls were very happy and her father Thomas was not far away with Gertrude. For the children it was an acute period of landscape imprinting and stimulated one of their primary concerns for the rest of their lives. This edge environment became their ideal place, which they would constantly refer to as their reference point for childhood perfection. Caroline's careful Pestalozzian home-schooled, 'head, heart and hands' outdoor-focused education of her children was far in advance of anything available to girls at the time. It created outstanding intellectual powers by exploring the natural world and testing the children's critical thinking by the lessons it offered. In ethical matters, love, empathy and friendship were vital alongside integrity and taking responsibility. Being outside and learning outdoors improved physical health but **Pestalozzi** also encouraged art, professionalism and social skills and all the abilities to make the world a better place. Caroline forbade them from reading any books that involved 'evil' as she wanted to show that the key principle of the world was 'goodness'. However, Caroline did not believe formal education should be commenced until at least sixteen; she maintained that students who preferred physical endeavour should not be made to pursue academic subjects and *vice versa*, as there was no point to it. Teaching with love and acknowledging and developing the talents of each child were her key to social progress.

Albert Einstein was also schooled in Pestalozzian methods, and indeed, because of the adoption of this form of education, Switzerland became illiteracy-free in 1830, long before the rest of Europe.

In 1849 Miranda started a career (at age 13) as a teacher and in 1851 the family moved to the dark, smoky, urban grime of Russell Place, Marylebone, London. Caroline had suggested the idea for someone to be paid to manage the Society for the Employment of Ladies (later the Ladies Cooperative Guild) and was delighted to be offered the post. This change was necessitated by the fact that her father Thomas, who had supported the family financially, had retired from his career as a practising (private) doctor in 1850 to work voluntarily for the new Board of Health. The move to inner London was another pivotal twist in the story; it created a sense of shock and awe, particularly in Octavia, as they experienced at first hand the true reality of devastating poverty and the ugliness surrounding destitution.

Caroline wrote, through articles in **Charles Dickens**' publication *Household Words*, about how her girls had settled in to wage earning in London. They worked at one of Mrs Wallace's bright ideas for poor children and supervised girls from the Ragged Schools making chintz and wire dolls-house toys. (Ragged Schools gave free but rudimentary evangelical 'education' to the poorest of children in Victorian industrial cities like London, Manchester and Edinburgh. These children were the most wretched of the destitute and wore ragged clothes. The schools were generally deemed to be failures by observers like **Charles Dickens** and **Henry Mayhew** and Parliament eventually agreed by passing the 1870 Education Act to provide compulsory schooling.) Caroline was clearly proud that newly teenaged Octavia had completely reorganised the lives of these Ragged School toy-workers (pooling a portion of their meagre earnings to ensure they all had a nutritious daily meal) and that Emily and Miranda were teaching them gardening, writing, geography and history. Caroline grew much prouder as her brood developed through their teens and, when her own Guild employment ceased, she was amazed that Octavia became the family organiser, book-keeper and minder for the repayment of James Hill's business debts. Caroline continued to work as a teacher and mingled with the radicals, artists, poets and influential friends to be found in the midst of the Quakers, Unitarians, Christian Socialists and her father's coterie of MPs, Lords and social reformers. Soon her girls grew into young women and were capable of holding their own conversations with such national and international luminaries as **Robert Browning**, **Hans Christian Andersen**, Charles Kingsley, **F D Maurice** and **John Ruskin**.

Caroline had strong and sure beliefs and struggled with anyone who sought to dominate her. One of her greatest battles was with the extraordinarily talented **Sophia Jex-Blake**, one of Octavia's closest friends. Of all Caroline's daughters, Octavia, in particular, had a habit of collecting friendships that replicated her closeness with her sisters, but she also had a tendency to hero-worship those who attracted her the most. Sometimes these were male intellectual 'missing father-figures' like Neale, **Maurice** or **Ruskin**, but they also included a series of larger-than-life young women like **Emma Cons** and **Sophia Jex-Blake** or the more easy-going such as **Emma Baumgartner**, Mary Harris and **Henrietta Barnett**.

It is clear from **Sophia Jex-Blake**'s diaries that for a while she enjoyed a passionate intimate relationship with Octavia. Matters came to a head when Sophia, a clever, wealthy, mercurial twenty year old who had summer-holidayed with Octavia in Wales, hatched a plan to live with the Hills. In 1860 Octavia threw herself into house-hunting to accommodate the expanded 'family plus Sophia' and picked 14 Nottingham Place, close to Regent's Park and not far from Queen's College where Sophia was teaching mathematics. During the summer of 1861 Octavia had been in the Lake District to be with Mary Harris who was struggling with illness. Confident Sophia sojourned in Nottingham Place whilst Octavia was still away and impressed her personality on Caroline. It seems that this did not go well and Caroline called Miranda and Emily back from Italy to assist in managing the household. Eventually Octavia was also summoned back by Caroline to make a stern and irrevocable choice: 'family' or Sophia. The outcome was inevitable and the stunned Sophia was dumped. There is a possibility that Sophia also had a crush on Miranda (or 'Frid' as she called her, and noted in her diary that it was an attraction initiated by Miranda) and perhaps Caroline just could not cope with the added emotional chaos.

After the seismic shock of the break-up with Octavia, Sophia's departure to Edinburgh triggered her astonishing and determined fight (quite literally, as the Surgeon's Hall Riots testify) to become one of the first female doctors in Britain. Meanwhile, Nottingham Place, with some whitewashing help from new best friend **Emma Cons**, eventually turned into a private school with Octavia, Miranda and Emily heading the basic teaching and Florence adding music and Italian, with Caroline as healthcare adviser. However, the death of Caroline's father in Italy in December 1861 stunned them all and Caroline left to go to Florence to mourn with her own sister Emily.

Caroline lived to be 94 and her intellectual powers were always sharp. She was the axle around which her daughters wheeled through life and the go-to person for advice and comfort in all matters. After the separation from James she was with one or more of her daughters at the centre of the family until the end.

'Life begins in happiness, and this instructs us how we ought to endeavour to continue.'

The children

JULIA HILL, 1819–1894 (first sibling)
Julia was born in North Brink, Wisbech, and died aged 75.

FREDERICK HILL, 1822–1822 (second sibling)
Born in North Brink, Wisbech, poor Frederick, like so many babies of the era, died as an infant.

LOUISA HILL, *c.*1822–*c.*1842 (third sibling)
Little is known about Louisa. She was born North Brink, Wisbech, and it is believed that she died aged about 20 in Bath.

MARGARET HILL, 'Margy', 1827–1924 (fourth sibling)
Margaret was born in Leverington, Norfolk, and died in June 1924 in Croydon aged 97. Although working as a teacher from her teens, Margaret tragically suffered complete blindness at the age of 20. As a responsible elder stepsister, and, by 1850, already established in running a small school in Boston with her sisters, Ida Eliza and Kate, she offered to take on Octavia as a trainee teacher when the financial support from Dr Southwood Smith was no longer available to aid Caroline and her daughters. In mid-life, in 1863, she married Andrew Whelpdale, 15 years her senior. As Mrs Whelpdale she is noted giving physics lectures at University College London to women including suffragists like Ada Wright. Despite being widowed and blind, Margaret managed to look after her aged father James Hill at her home in Sydenham, Kent until his death in 1872. In 1891 Margy was present with Caroline, Miranda, Octavia and Florence, as well as with Emily and Maurice Lewes, at one of the Hill family Christmas gatherings.

ARTHUR HILL, 1829–1909 (fifth sibling)
The second child of Eliza Jecks and James Hill was born on 27 March 1829 in the distinctive riverside house by the wharves in Wisbech. He was just three when his mother died and six when his father married Caroline.

In 1840, when Arthur was 11, and under James and Caroline's caring guidance, he was sent to be educated at the **Pestalozzi**

Arthur Hill, Mayor of Reading (1883–1887) and civic philanthropist, posthumously honoured by the Arthur Hill Memorial Baths in 1911.

School on Potter Street in Worksop run by Dr Benjamin Hildenmaier, and was there in 1841 when his stepmother was in Hampstead with his stepsisters. Worksop at that time was a great centre for private education institutions and the reputation of the **Pestalozzi** School was of the highest. Pupils from this school, such as William and George Spencer, were later leaders of a public education revolution in teaching methods in Britain. These methods and the values that were inculcated in pupils are critical clues to understanding how this small family of Pestalozzi-influenced Hill children were enabled to achieve the things they did in later life. The concept of 'head, heart and hand' helped pupils learn by observing nature outdoors through local landscapes and experimenting with handicrafts to understand how industry worked. In such a physically healthy environment the addition of acquiring excellent moral values and social lessons completed the trilogy of essential life-skill qualities.

In 1851, now aged 22, Arthur was recorded in the census as living in Boston, Lincolnshire, having completed his education and possibly an apprenticeship in railway construction. His occupation is recorded as 'clerk to railway contractor'. However, although unmarried and ostensibly living alone in digs he was not removed from the strong Hill family circle. His teacher sisters Margaret, Ida Eliza and Kate resided at another address in Boston at the same time, running a small school.

Arthur was involved in providing the infrastructure of the great Victorian Railway Mania funded by the speculation of frantic investors in the rapid and seemingly never-ending network of railways. Many of these lines went to places that would never make a profit from the shipment of scant agricultural produce or scarce passengers. Some of this mad speculation was fuelled by the government of the day giving extraordinary amounts of 'compensation deemed to be owed' to British slave-owners on the abolition of slavery. As this sum of £20 million, the equivalent of £16.5 *billion* in today's values, or 40 per cent of the then Treasury's entire annual spending budget, became available to 'slave-deprived' claimants in the mid to late 1830s, some of the cash was put into acquiring fine houses and estates and some into railway speculation. The railway bubble foamed to its highest point in 1844–46 when an astonishing 6000 miles of railways were authorised by Parliament to be built. These authorised railways were being built through the 1850s and 1860s as the companies called in the promissory shares of the speculators. As most shares were bought on a 10 per cent deposit basis in the expectation of quick gains, the companies' call on shareholders to pay the 90 per cent owed caused ruin to many of these naively greedy investors.

Arthur Hill worked for Morton Peto, a risky, opportunistic contract builder who had not only constructed Nelson's Column in Trafalgar Square, parts of the new Houses of Parliament and the London Brick Sewer (prompted by the sanitary reforms of Dr Thomas Southwood Smith) but also moved into railway development. He built the impressive Greek-temple-style Curzon Street Station in Birmingham in 1838 (now allocated as part of the new railway terminus station for High Speed 2) and the Hanwell to Langley section of the Great Western Railway (GWR), including Wharncliffe Viaduct. Peto was also working with Thomas Brassey on contracts for the Great Northern Railway (GNR), where ingenious solutions had to be found for building lines across the sodden peatland Fens in East Anglia.

It is possible that Arthur had been working on these GNR projects in and around Boston. Peto also continued to develop work for the GWR (including the building of Reading Station 1840–41) and this connection might have first brought Reading to the attention of Arthur Hill. Around 1848, his father James, now ill (see p. 16), cited Arthur as the addressee for any requests for shares in the National Land and Buildings Association at 2 Bartlett's Buildings, Holborn, London.

In December 1852, Arthur married Harriet Ann Tuck, the daughter of a Norfolk butcher from Shipdham. He had also left Peto to join a new business and arrived in Reading to work as a coal merchant for John Marshall's Great Western Coal Company established the previous year. By 1857 Arthur was the managing clerk but John Marshall, who was not the best of businessmen and despite making a fortune transporting emigrants to Australia, in that year suffered his third bankruptcy. Although he was only 28, Arthur's offer to buy the company was accepted and he found himself as the owner of a string of railway coal merchant depots. This was the midst of the era when coal was king of the fuels and the railways were making it accessible to everyone. Following Marshall's lead, Arthur Hill also won a contract with the Colonial Land & Emigration Commission as 'H.M. Emigration Agent for Berkshire' to provide passage to South Australia via Plymouth. There was big money to be made for agents from the government's trade in boat people.

Harriet and Arthur had a family of three children by 1857 (Arthur William born 1854, Frederick Charles born 1856 and Harriet Kate born 1857) and lived at 1 Baker Street, Reading. By 1861, managing not only an expanding business but also an expanding family, they were resident with three servants at 39 Friar Street, Reading. The Hills had another four children (Thomas Edward born 1859 and Gertrude Louisa born 1860, who were followed by Henry Ernest born 1863 and Constance Ida born 1865). Arthur Hill bought other coal and coke depots alongside the railway network and added coal gas as a product. The successful young coal merchant seized the opportunity to expand to station yards at Blackwater, Camberley, Oxford, Wokingham, Sunningdale and Wellington College. The latter station location (later renamed Crowthorne) was sufficiently attractive, as a new settlement in the countryside, to lure the Hills out of Reading and by 1868 the family were residing next to the College (newly established in 1859) in a big house with gardens called 'Heatherside'.

Affluence, business standing and a position in the community followed and contemporary references noted that the Hills were hosting fund-raising events to collect money for the new village church and new village school. The male children were receiving education, some at school in Wellington College or Blenheim House (and later Rugby School), whilst the girls were being educated within the extended family of Pestalozzi-trained teachers. Principal amongst these teachers was Arthur's stepmother Caroline and stepsister Miranda, and in 1871 Harriet Kate was being educated at the Marylebone home school in London. Meanwhile in Kent (Sydenham) Arthur's younger stepsister Ida Eliza (now Mrs Paddock) was home-schooling Gertrude Louisa with four other pupils. Octavia Hill visited Arthur in 1868 when he asked her to be godmother to Constance Ida and, over the following years, gradually got to know her new nieces and nephews. However, this settled domesticity perturbed Octavia, and, in a letter to Mary Harris, wrote that it was 'strange to me' but added that 'the children's confidence in their father's love and strength, his joy in helping and planning and working for them, brings tears into my eyes'. Was this perhaps a haunting memory of the absence of their father, James, affecting Octavia emotionally and acting as a stimulant to Arthur to provide domestic security?

Octavia was not slow to suggest that Arthur should host some of her Ragged School children from London's poorest housing to get a taste of fresh air and natural beauty, and sent several groups to the luxurious surroundings of 'Heatherside' (see p. 46). She also counselled Arthur against becoming an MP for Reading, thinking there was little noble in being a parliamentarian.

In 1879 Arthur was elected as Conservative councillor for Church Ward in Reading and soon began work on improvements to the town's drains and sewage-related sanitation issues (see Thomas Southwood Smith, p. 9). Using his business skills he forged a new way of dealing with Reading's public accounts and was instrumental in the success of the Reading Corporation Act of 1881. Arthur and family had moved back to Reading from Crowthorne before 1881 and were living on 76 acres at Elm Lodge on Oxford Road, where local business directories described him as a 'merchant and farmer'.

In 1883 the post of Mayor of Reading was offered to Arthur, and retained each year until 1887. The freedom of the role allowed Arthur to use his heart to demonstrate his public-spiritedness, doing publicly advantageous land deals, extending Reading's borders, giving land on Oxford Road for St Mark's Church, paying for a marble bust of Reading's biscuit entrepreneur William Palmer, establishing the Children's Library, and making possible free concerts in the Town Hall and even early closing days for the workers in shops and banks. His stand-out gift, however, was the purchase (for £300) of the only full-size, 230-foot-long replica of the Bayeux Tapestry in the world. This incredible embroidery is now securely housed in Reading Museum where all visitors can freely view it. The work itself has connections to **William Morris** and the town of Leek in Staffordshire and, like the story of the marble frieze looted from the Parthenon in Greece by Lord Elgin between 1801 and 1812, it was suggested by a perhaps tongue-in-cheeky Leeky, in the early twenty-first century, that the tapestry should be 'repatriated' to Leek.

The idea behind the making of the English copy of the Bayeux Tapestry began in 1816 when Charles Stothard went to Bayeux to meticulously record the entire work as a full size drawing, which was then engraved. The engravings were then coloured and wax impressions made of the stitching and recorded in plaster casts. By 1822 the complete apparatus to make a copy had been assembled by the Society of Antiquaries. It was not until 1875, however, that a number of critical threads in the story started to come together. Elizabeth Wardle, wife of Thomas Wardle (a leading silk manufacturer and dye chemist from Hencroft Dye Works) made the acquaintance of **William Morris**, who was searching for natural dyes (made from weld, walnuts, madder and woad) for his Arts and Crafts Movement products. The introductions were made via Thomas's younger brother George who was an employee in Morris & Co. in London. Morris was fascinated by the Middle Ages, owned a set of the Bayeux Tapestry etchings, and had already visited Bayeux with fellow Pre-Raphaelite Brotherhood painter Edward Burne-Jones to study the real thing. Morris stayed with the Wardles in Staffordshire and amongst the dinnertime dye discussions the possibility of someone recreating the tapestry (really an embroidery) as 'England's copy' must have been aired.

In 1879 Elizabeth organised the Leek Embroidery School as a showcase for the Wardle's commercial venture in producing embroidery kits (for middle-class ladies with nothing else to do). By

1885 the decision seems to have been made by the Wardles that a copy of the Bayeux Tapestry would be a perfect public relations puff for their products. Elizabeth set to work organising 35 female members of the school to embroider it using the Society of Antiquaries' facsimiles as guidance, 100 pounds of wool and all the natural dyes that a medieval embroiderer would have used, taken from the Hencroft Dye Works. The women were paid by foot of completed embroidery and clearly some were keener than others (Anne Smith Endon completed 20 feet) but all contributors had their names recorded on the final panel as well as 'their' sections. Elizabeth Wardle oversaw the whole project from inception, in early 1885, to display in Leek on 14 June 1886. It toured the UK and the USA and was an outstanding success.

Some of Arthur Hill's children were still living at home in the 1880s, but soon after they married locally or dispersed to Australia, India and Italy. Gertrude Louisa married **Dr Jamieson Body Hurry** and lived in Reading. The youngest daughter, Constance Ida, died in Italy at San Remo at the age of 22 and the eldest son, Arthur William, returned from Australia but died in 1896.

In retirement Arthur handed the coal and gas business to son Thomas, who carried this work on until 1925 from his home in Caversham.

Arthur died at the age of 79 at Erleigh Court in Reading on 16 February 1909. He was buried with his wife at Shere in Surrey. Son Frederick had come back from India with his wife in 1893 to be vicar for Shere parish and established a suitable place for family memorials. There is a stained glass memorial to Harriet Hill, Arthur's wife, in Shere church. Frederick also attended at the burial of Miranda Hill.

After being heaped from on high with accolades and praise from the civic burghers and people of Reading, Arthur's family began the process of selecting a suitable public memorial to his life. Arthur had been involved in several sporting activities and immediate attention was given to suggestions to encourage future generations. In the end his son in law, **Dr Jamieson Body Hurry**, offered to purchase land near Cemetery Junction to build the Arthur Hill Memorial Baths.

The building, including six individual bathtubs for those who had none at home, opened to the public on 29 November 1911. After over one hundred years of use by generations of local people, the Memorial Baths were deemed by Reading Borough Council to be too expensive to maintain and the baths were closed in December 2016, despite a huge local outcry and campaign to save them. In March 2017 campaigners threw in the towel despite raising £10,000 to form a community interest company to take over the running of the facility. Now the only memorial to Reading's much-loved former mayor is in Kent. When Octavia Hill died in 1912, Dr Hurry also prudently purchased 39 acres of land in Arthur's memory at One Tree Hill, near Sevenoaks, to join the suite of the earliest National Trust open space acquisitions.

IDA ELIZA HILL, 1831–1899 (sixth sibling)
After working in the school in Boston, Ida Eliza married Francis William Paddock in 1862 and lived in Lewisham (then part of Kent), where she developed another school for girls attended by the daughters of Arthur Hill from Reading.

KATE HILL, 1832–1851 (seventh sibling)
Not much is known about Kate's life and early death. At some point she had attempted to involve Miranda in her interests in the Peace Society (the Society for the Promotion of Permanent and Universal Peace, founded in June 1816) because Miranda fired off a series of questions about what the Society stood for and how it might be helped. It is possible that there was an early Wisbech connection as Priscilla Hannah Peckover's Quaker Women's peace group had over 4000 members in the Wisbech area. Kate was recorded in letters as being in Uttoxeter and working as a teacher in a school in Boston, Lincolnshire, with her sisters Margaret and Ida Eliza at the time of the census in 1851, the year she died.

MIRANDA HILL, 'Andy', 1836–1910 (eighth sibling)
Miranda was born on 1 January 1836 in Wisbech, Cambridgeshire; she died unmarried on 31 May 1910 in Marylebone, London. Miranda was the sweetest and cheeriest of all the daughters born to Caroline

Hill. Her mother described Miranda's state of mind as 'dreamy' and 'poetic' and her imagination always flew to sunnier places. Even in the grimiest of grim corners Miranda could see the lighter side (and, as a child, 'fairies'). Although never formally schooled herself, but well versed in Pestalozzian educational thinking by Caroline Hill, her calling as a teacher quickly developed from 1849 onwards.

In 1851, Caroline Hill, as ever anxious that the family should attempt to cover its costs, spotted the opportunity presented by 'Mrs Wallace's patented consolidated glass' – a new philanthropic glass-painting business for 'economically distressed' ladies. The artistic Octavia and the dreamy Miranda might therefore be able to work together, but before they could start, Mr Vansittart Neale of the Christian Socialists acquired the business. As strange as it might seem, this was a pivotal point in history. Without the encounter with the Christian Socialists Miranda would have gone to join Margaret Hill at her school and Octavia would have worked with Margaret Gilles as a trainee artist and the family would have fragmented further. Moreover, the Christian Socialists wanted a manager for this new business, which was to be run through their Ladies Cooperative Guild. The reputation of Caroline's father, Thomas Southwood Smith, secured Caroline the job and everyone moved to the dark reality of working-class London. Octavia was deeply and irrevocably shocked by the destitution, and the shock ignited the spark for social and environmental justice that thereafter dominated her life and helped formulate the whispery thoughts that things could only get better. Miranda was the joker, and teased her younger sister with a touch of gallows humour by writing a fake headstone epitaph for herself with Octavia as the fake author:

'Her foibles were many, her virtues were few
And the more she laughed, the more stern the world grew'

In 1846 Thomas Southwood Smith and Gertrude had moved to 'Hillside' in Highgate, then in the countryside fringe of London with views over Caen Woods, Lord Mansfield's Park and a collection of pony fields, hay meadows and apple orchards; a perfect outdoor playground not only for Gertrude but also all her visiting sisters including Miranda and Octavia.

Modern research into cultural landscapes has shown that there is a global archetype landscape that all humans tend to prefer when offered a choice in tests. This image of a preferential aspect of a landscape includes features of bluish-green with trees, open areas with paths leading to the horizon, water, people and animals. It does not matter whether you are from Iceland or Kenya, as your preference will be the same and peculiarly *not* conditioned by where you live. It is called the 'savannah hypothesis' and postulates a genetic memory of the landscape from which modern human stock developed. All these landscape features were present at both Finchley and Hillside, with the bluish hills of the far-off Surrey Downs and green pathways to them becoming a reference point for all of Miranda and Octavia's later dreaming and theorising about open spaces and Green Belts. This preference seems to be hard-wired into our brains but requires a timely stimulus to activate it before it fully engages.

Additional research by Gordon Howell Orians and Judith Heerwagen in the 1990s and Stephen and Rachel Kaplan in the 1980s has refined these landscape preferences by including complexity over homogeneity and even climbable trees with limbs close to the ground. Further peculiarity was added by Balling and Falk's experiments in 2010 with landscape preferences for 'living in' and 'just visiting' tested on various age groups from eight to eighty. The experiments showed mixed results but *not for the eight-year-olds*, who all selected the 'savannah' landscape for both visiting and living, although none had any experience of it.

In 1846 Miranda was ten and Octavia was eight. Hillside's landscape must have been a significant factor in the Hill sisters' obsessive drive to develop the concepts of urban open spaces, urban fringe Green Belts and places far away to enjoy air and exercise. It was if an unconscious switch had been turned on in their heads.

In 1875 Miranda published a book that included a fairy story called the 'Fairy-spinner' with the Pestalozzian theme of courtly knights who, instead of slaying dragons to win the princess (who was studious and opinionated as well as beautiful), had to, as well as being fit, be highly educated, understand Latin and Greek literature, be *specifically* learned in natural sciences and be able to tell 'what the snail under the strawberry leaf was thinking'. This impossible 'snail test', as the book calls it, is probably a Hill sisters joke, as they both kept pet snails in their bedrooms. After many other tests of character for both knight *and* princess it all ends happily. The second moralistic story, 'Out of Date or Not?' has the paranormal theme of a guardian knight of old returning to the inter-penetrable space of the present to witness the chivalrous battles against the evils of 'disease, crime and ignorance'. Many of these evils, the by-products of blackened industrial towns, are being fought not by medieval swords and lances but by the provision of better sanitation, sunny playgrounds, workshops, schools and happy teachers. This was the Southwood Smith–Hill family soap-opera plot.

In December 1875 Miranda made history (although she did not know it) by making up another imaginative little exercise for her poor students just to help current and former pupils understand their lives better and how they might be changed by the application of 'beauty'. It was originally called 'To those who love beauty'. Miranda had written it stimulated by something that (the not impoverished) Samuel Barnett had said:

> 'It is not poverty that is such a weight that is upon everybody in the East End, it is the ugliness.'

In typical Hill family fashion Miranda, and **Robert Hunter**'s sister Dorothy, had been thinking about starting up a little group of friends to work on the idea, albeit one she grandly called the Society for the Diffusion of Beauty, but a delighted Octavia saw its wider potential and enthusiastically grabbed it. Octavia had the paper published and disseminated.

At this juncture the wild ideas and the organisational force combined together to unleash much of what became the future National Trust, civic societies, Open Space Movement and even the Clean Air activists.

The impact of the publication of Miranda's revised paper, called *'Those who love Beautiful Things'*, as distributed and promoted by Octavia, was immediate. Relaxing in the warm bath of praise, Miranda was persuaded by Octavia to present it to a meeting of the National Health Society. In the room were sympathetic and influential people and although the Society for the Diffusion of Beauty was to mutate shortly afterwards its spirit lived on and developed. The name Kyrle Society had been suggested after the meeting by one Benjamin Nattalie and was swiftly adopted.

Miranda had originally set out its purposes to be

'to learn as far as I can what has been done and what wants doing in the way of beautifying in poor districts, to write a short account every month, and to send it to the members of this society.'

To be a member of the Kyrle Society all you had to do was be interested; there were no fees to pay or meetings to attend although donations were very welcome. As it transpired there were many people who were interested and some of them were either rich or influential or both. Thanks to the poem 'Of the Use of Riches' by Alexander Pope, the name of **John Kyrle**, or in Pope's words 'The Man of Ross', had become a literary icon of selflessness and good deeds in improving the quality of life in Ross-on-Wye, Herefordshire, for his fellow citizens. This was the model that many Christian Socialists wished to follow and the Kyrle Society had arrived with splendid good timing, ideas, leadership and abundant opportunities for betterment.

The Hills and their keenest Kyrlesque supporters jumped into action immediately to bring more 'sweetness and light into the homes of the poor'. Wild flowers were collected by the bundle and distributed into poor houses; small gardens were laid out where feasible and planted up; 'happy evenings' were organised in boarding schools; choirs were brigaded to sing or give singing lessons and the vacuum of blank walls was filled with uplifting slogans. Octavia was particularly keen to put up a huge slogan on a wall next to Waterloo Station to declare to the masses:

'Do noble deeds'

Where she and Miranda could take direct action they engineered it and, in one instance, oversaw the sponsorship of tiles to be put along the frontage of the slum property in Freshwater Place, Marylebone, acquired with the help of **John Ruskin**. These De Morgan tiles were to be crafted in true Ruskinian fashion and would spell out:

'Every house is builded by some man, but He that built all things is God'

– with each tile paid for by a philanthropic sponsor. Sadly the frost got to them and they later dropped off. After this initial burst of activity and appreciative feedback more voices and more money were added to the infant Kyrle Society. Octavia applied her book-keeping skills as Treasurer and Miranda continued the many tasks to 'diffuse a love of beautiful things among our poor brethren'.

With so many new ideas being proposed it was agreed to set up four different sub-committees to further work in each direction: open spaces, literature distribution, musical and decorative. The latter continued the moralising murals work but also brought works of art to hospitals and other institutions, whilst religious music was surreally ushered into the world of the destitute by a touring choir singing oratorios. In a world without public libraries the literary group dropped books off in working men's clubs, mechanics institutes, schools and hospitals, whilst the open spacers set about opening up disused graveyards. This branch was set up in 1879 with **Robert Hunter** as chairman and added to the existing work of the Commons Preservation Society.

The simplicity of Miranda's idea was its great strength; if the poor could not afford to travel to see the beauty of nature and greenery in the urban fringes then it should be brought to them. It was a beautiful if preposterously ambitious idea. It started with the throwing open of disused churchyards in the grimiest of neighbourhoods, the only places where there was any hope of creating an open space or a hint of greenery where the poor might freely gather. Burial grounds in St George's in the East, Drury Lane, St John's Waterloo Road and St Giles at Seven Dials were opened and planted up with greenery.

Schemes to do the same in the Quaker burial grounds of Bunhill failed and the owner of Mile End Road could not be persuaded to create a wide tree-lined boulevard (although the Luftwaffe shelped to bring this idea to fruition of sorts much, much later as Mile End Park).

A very vocal enthusiast for the decorative branch was **William Morris**, aided by the first female architect, Lady Mary Lovelace, and he spoke to the working classes with a passion for the project that rose above his normal cantankerous style. In the smoky cities of the north the Kyrle's branches grew twigs and bore fruit. In mercantile Liverpool and industrial Manchester the movement expanded into the forerunner of civic societies. In Liverpool this went as far as Mrs Birt's Sheltering Homes but also had a focus on clean air, street trees, pocket gardens and disused graveyards, and, by the end of the century helped to acquire Bidston Hill in the Wirral to prevent development. Back in London a horticultural branch developed into the Invalid Children's Aid Society in 1908 and the Kyrle spawned the Metropolitan Public Garden, Boulevards and Playgrounds Association in 1882 with Kyrle Society member Lord Reginald Brabazon. The Association, which shortened its title in 1885, dedicated itself to 'giving to the people gardens and to the children playgrounds' and was the keenest body in implementing the 1881 Metropolitan Open Spaces Act and helping local authorities care for burial grounds. These ideas developed teeth with the 1884 Disused Burial Grounds Act, which prevented them being built on and permitted their use as pocket parks for the poor. By 1893 the Association had notched up 82 burial grounds, and 116 playgrounds, and had planted 2400 trees, supplied 100 seats and erected 18 fountains.

In 1884 a bigger test was the purchase of Parliament Hill. This has now become an iconic film location for panoramic views of London and has featured in *The Omen, Run Fatboy Run* and *Notes on a Scandal.* In Miranda's day it was sometimes known as Traitor's Hill as it was the vantage point selected by Guy Fawkes and Robert Catesby to watch the Houses of Parliament blow up. In 1884 it was on sale for £300,000 and, following the Metropolitan Board of Works' acquisition of adjacent Hampstead Heath, public awareness was high and the Board was pressed to stump up most of the money, leaving the Hill sisters £52,500 to raise privately. Octavia's view was straightforward:

> 'I should like to see some of the rich of London proud to share the remaining part of a gift which will be, so far as we can see, a great and lasting and a visible blessing for thousands.'

When the large garden of the Fawcett's house in Vauxhall came on the market in 1887, following the early death of former Postmaster General Henry Fawcett, the Kyrle Society saw it as a chance to have a new public open space south of the Thames. Henry and Millicent Fawcett (the suffragist) were connected to the Commons Preservation Society via **Robert Hunter**, who was at one time solicitor to the General Post Office, so fund-raising and negotiations advanced swiftly. Local working-class people held an open-air meeting that Miranda and Octavia attended. Florence Nightingale wrote a 'beautiful letter' about the cause and in just three years the money was raised, landscaping completed and the park called 'The Lawn' opened by the Prince of Wales and **Princess Louise**. Octavia was moved to write:

> 'and now it is done: and for long years as long as our people need it and wish for it, flowers will grow and sunlight have leave to penetrate there.'

Burnham Beeches is a 540-acre outpost of the beech woodlands on the dip slope of the Chiltern Hills that were once draped across the landscape surrounding the northern flanks of the town that became Slough. It is woodland of veteran pollard beech and oak trees of prodigious size and majesty. In the 1870s developers saw it as the perfect place to create large suburban villas close to the Great Western railway line. It was undoubtedly 'beautiful' and therefore a chance for Miranda and the Kyrle Society to get involved. Due to the earlier legislative work of the Commons Preservation Society, the Corporation of the City of London was enabled to acquire commons within a 25-mile radius of St Paul's at the heart of the city. Burnham Beeches were just within their grasp but not all of the woods were still common land. Moreover, the Open Spaces Act 1878 did not allow the purchase of former common areas, so Sir Henry Peek (the 'godfather' of the Garibaldi biscuit and local MP) bought them to give to the City of London. In 1880 the Coal, Corn and Finance Committee of the Corporation used taxes charged against the movement of such commodities to fund the acquisition, and the common is still open and managed by the Corporation today. It has also been used as a film set for *Goldfinger, Robin Hood, Prince of Thieves* and two *Harry Potter* films and is now a Site of Special Scientific Interest.

Miranda continued to gently push for women's acceptance onto public committees and other parts of civic life. She was elated to be elected to be a member of the Marylebone Board of Guardians in 1895 to look after the poor, and delighted by Octavia's belated appointment to the Royal Commission on Poor Law in 1905. Her quiet interventions for others often went unremarked but when Octavia returned to a house filled with the scent of daffodils it was as a result of a gift from the mother of a sickly boy from the workhouse for both of whom Miranda had managed to find employment on the Isles of Scilly, far away from the deadly London smog. The mother was convinced it had saved his life. Augustus Smith, their employer, was known to the Hills as 'Lord of the Isles'. He had unfenced the illegally fenced Berkhamsted Common during a daring night raid by a trainload of navvies set up by the Commons Preservation Society, and was then bringing bulb growing to the Isles of Scilly as an economic activity to reduce poverty.

In her later years, from 1903–1906, Miranda continued writing and publishing her plays and books of fairy stories before her illness and death in 1910.

GERTRUDE HILL, 1837–1923 (ninth sibling)

Gertrude was born in Wisbech on 28 July 1837 and died in March 1923 in Paddington, London. She was only three when her parents gave her up for adoption to Caroline's father and from 1840 to 1842 she lived in Kentish Town with Thomas Southwood Smith. Thereafter they moved to the idyllic setting of 'Hillside' on the borders of Hampstead Heath and Swiss Cottage Common. Here they entertained many guests and her sisters frequently came to visit, sometimes with children from the Ragged School and later with slum tenants. Gertrude and Miranda were listening to Professor Richard Owen talking about mosses near Hampstead Heath, when a gang of bedraggled children led by Octavia in a battered hat burst through a hedge, chatted briefly and then vanished towards the grimy city carrying armfuls of bluebells. In 1878, before she went to Europe with **Harriot Yorke**, Octavia confessed to Gertrude, 'I am confident that my work in the houses will not really suffer in my absence; but my open spaces will miss me, for nobody knows they are there.' Some have attributed Octavia with the first use of the term 'open spaces'.

Gertrude was the only Hill sister who actually got married (in March 1865) *and* had children. Her husband Charles Lee Lewes – born in 1842, died aged 49 in Luxor, Egypt – was the stepson of 'George Eliot'. Gertrude's three daughters, Elinor, Blanche and Maud, in turn all married and started their own families within her lifetime. Elinor acted as Octavia's secretary before and after she married Carrington Ouvry until she became a mother, and Octavia became godmother to Elinor's second son Romilly. All the aunts bestowed gifts and good wishes on the expanding family; Octavia visited her nearest older sister after Gertrude's girls had left home and until she followed her ageing grandfather to his retirement home at The Pines in Weybridge.

Gertrude wrote a comprehensive record of the life of her grandfather and his achievements in public health and sanitation reform, which she dedicated to her mother. She was one of the sensible sisters who picked up the pieces when Octavia had one of her periodic breakdowns and needed to rest, often abroad, for long periods with Harriot Yorke, or on one of her frequent visits to the hydrotherapeutic spa centre of Ben Rhydding on Ilkley Moor.

OCTAVIA HILL, 'Ockey', 1838–1912 (eighth daughter, tenth sibling)
Octavia was born on 3 December 1838 in Wisbech and died unmarried on 13 August 1912. She enjoyed a happy outdoor childhood at Finchley filled with inventive play, exploration, observation of nature and undoubtedly, as manifest throughout her later life, a heavy degree of landscape imprinting from their unofficial 'playground', Swiss Cottage Fields. Many of her open space endeavours, particularly with Miranda, make reference back to these idealistic places, the sun-filled Finchley commons and Hampstead heaths. They were an important motivating factor for both sisters and demonstrate a key point in the psychological development of human beings everywhere; the provision of accessible wild play spaces for children is a critical issue in rounded childhood growth. Having such space and freedom creates better-adjusted adults as Richard Louv has ably demonstrated in his book *Last Child in the Woods*.

Octavia enjoyed much laughter but there was also some deep sadness and seriousness in her demeanour. It seems feasible, alongside her several nervous breakdowns, that these unfortunate mental health susceptibilities might have been inherited from her father. However, she seems to have balanced that with an inheritance of his boundless energy. When not playing, the sisters would be learning, with the grace of good students given freedom to be interested in learning by their exceptional teacher-mother, Caroline. Octavia grew particularly fond of poetry and the classics and read endlessly, absorbing more and more detail. Religion was also hugely important to her and much debated and referenced in all her letters and writings, with much praising and reverence for God. The strong religious element in her philosophy guided her, as it did many of her fellow Victorians, through times of unremitting hardships and crises. Although she did entertain doubts about the purpose of creation at the most extreme points of personal challenge, she seems to have kept her faith intact and relied upon it for self-help. Many branches of Unitarian dissenters, as well as East End Jewish populations and a small number of serene Quakers, surrounded her but although attracted to the peacefulness of Quakerism and its adherents, like her early best friend Mary Harris, she went to the Church of England aided by **FD Maurice** for her version of Christianity. She was also attracted to girls her own age like **Emma Baumgartner**, who had stable, comfortably well-off family situations; something she craved.

Octavia worked hard during 1856 learning the craft of book-keeping and, at 18, running the affairs of the Ragged School children's toy-making workshop. This was a commercial enterprise that required receipts and expenditure to be balanced perfectly, goods sold and materials paid for, as well as ensuring that client orders were fulfilled and reputation maintained. However, Octavia and Miranda made it part schooling too. It was a test-run for everything that followed in her social housing schemes because she insisted on the simplest of rules but strict adherence. Getting to know the impecunious school workforce and the details of their benighted lives was a crucial part of assessing their moral worth as child workers. A meticulous form of cataloguing and recording became an obsession with Octavia and permeated every enterprise she touched thereafter. At times Octavia took it upon herself to track down absent child-workers and she would stumble down ladders into the domestic black coalholes that some of them lived in. Suitably chastened by these horrors, her active mind was quick to formulate remedies. Even though helping single individuals was never going to make much of a dent in the morbidity tables of the time, her family passion for reform, if not alms-giving, was stirred. The Ragged School toy-makers persisted with Emily's help until 1857.

The family move to Russell Place in Marylebone had thus precipitated much teenage angst and soul-searching about the conditions of the poor and destitute. Octavia, being particularly affected by this, sought meaning from it, with her main target for questions being God. It was inevitable that meeting radical preachers like **FD Maurice** would help shape some of the answers in a young and malleable intellect. Octavia couldn't get enough of Maurice's sermons and his mission to Christianise the socialists. Maurice, like **Owen**, saw capitalism and competition as unchristian but his sermons were more about Christian brotherhood than socialist politics. Inevitably, there were many disagreements among the Christian Socialists and a period of dormancy was followed by a revival in the 1880s and the rise of the Independent Labour Party.

John Ruskin visited the Ladies Cooperative Guild with **F D Maurice** in 1853 and first met the Hill sisters there, when Octavia was just fifteen. He was no doubt impressed by their precocious knowledge, enthusiasm and youthful idealism. At the time he was in the midst of his scandalous public divorce from Effie Gray. Ruskin offered to employ Octavia as a copyist in his art book business where she raised additional household income for the next ten and a half years working on the *Seven Lamps of Architecture* and *Modern Painters V.* She found herself working alongside a succession of other teenage girls that Ruskin creepily described as 'his pets'. Octavia ignored these warning signs as she succumbed to Ruskin-worship, craving his attention. If he praised her when she worked for him in Denmark Hill, she would sing out loud as she tramped back across London. Octavia may have unconsciously copied his style of writing and speaking and she certainly absorbed his messages to the world as he rose to become one of the greatest art critics and thinkers of his age.

Ruskin was a genius polymath and as a very wealthy man, following the death of his father in 1864, he could afford to follow wherever his whimsy or intellectual desires led him. Like **William Morris**, he was deeply desirous to show that industrialism could be defeated by a return to non-industrial days of craft, natural processes and honest work. He backed a variety of ventures that gave life to his ideals, including cooperative communal farming near Sheffield for ex-industrial workers. He created the Guild of St George to act as a platform for this and a museum in Sheffield that he festooned with minerals and natural objects of beauty from his personal collection. He later influenced and part-funded the remarkable Oxford Museum of Natural History. Ruskin, however, was generally impractical and unable to cope, and often sent his agents and even his gardener to rescue his Quixotic deals from flopping. One such bizarre event was the digging of a road between Upper and Lower Hinksey, two rustic villages near Oxford. **Ruskin** conceived a plan to counter the distasteful introduction of competitive sports at Oxford University by doing something useful and noble with fit young men instead. In 1874 he bagged a motley crew of undergraduates including **Hardwicke Rawnsley**, Oscar Wilde, Arnold Toynbee and Alfred Milner to dig a track and plant wildflower verges. They stuck at it through two wet winter months before Ruskin disappeared to Venice and even his gardener could not complete the task; only half a road was ever built.

In summer 1859 Octavia made a new lifelong friend in **Emma Baumgartner** and after the slightest encouragement from Emma went to see her family home in Godmanchester, Huntingdonshire. She discovered that, seemingly, they had much in common. Emma even taught Octavia to row on the Cam and they shared a happy interest in Ruskin and other personal intimacies. Emma never married and always donated money to Octavia's causes, including constantly impressive annual donations to the National Trust until she died.

Mary Harris, a Quaker living in the Lake District, was one of Octavia's most trusted confidantes and they exchanged dozens of letters on all manner of issues, often with a religious focus, as well as irregular personal visits in times of crisis.

Early in 1860, twenty-one-year-old Octavia started giving book-keeping lessons to the flamboyant and hugely talented mathe-matician **Sophia Jex-Blake**. They spent Easter 1860 at the Jex-Blake family holiday home in Betws-y-Coed in Snowdonia. For Sophia it blossomed into love. It was also Octavia's first sight of mountains and the double romance of it all made her return home giddy, as Sophia noted in a letter to her mother on 30 July 1860:

'...Octavia looks five years younger and as bright as a sunbeam'.

The leasing of the house together in Nottingham Place, Marylebone, followed this moment of joy. Although by October 1861 Sophia was forced to leave Octavia and departed for Edinburgh, she never forgot her. Despite the emotional traumas of Sophia's abrupt departure and the death of Octavia's beloved grandfather in December 1861 she continued to work for Ruskin, to teach at the London Ladies College and to develop Nottingham Place as a school.

When Ruskin was in an elated mood, he was capable of accelerating ideas that moved him and when in 1864, Octavia suggested her pioneering social housing enterprise to improve the lives of the deserving poor, he agreed to lend her money. There were strings attached (as he had also mused about whether he should invest in Great Consols stocks instead – see **William Morris**, p.91) but provided he made a 5 per cent annual return on capital, even from these impoverished tenants, Ruskin was content to let her try buying slum properties to do up. This was Octavia's first big moment, to prove her theories on bettering the lives of the working classes by creating healthier and more beautiful home environments, so that they could then apply themselves to self-improvement. It was a touch of strong and stable household governance probably based on **Samuel Smiles'** book *Self-Help* published in 1859, someone known to her father and mother from their time in Leeds.

Thus, with the help of Ruskin's deep pockets, in April 1865 Octavia bought the lease of Paradise Place (now Garbutt Place) and later Freshwater Place, ironically named versions of small slum hellholes in Marylebone. Her improvements were duly made but if she had been uninterested in recording her struggles, history might not have noticed these tiny boosts to slum housing improvements. The critical fact of her accountancy obsession was that Octavia recorded everything, exhaustively, and wrote about it continuously. This was a new middle-class fashion stimulated perhaps by Ruskin (who has been called the world's first blogger) and his weekly, semi-narcissistic publication *Fors Clavigera*. Octavia published her annual *Letter to Fellow Workers* in part to instruct her growing band of female volunteer rent collectors and also as a means of recording her thoughts.

In the manner of the age, these newsletters, as stuffy as their style might be, went viral and news spread upwards amongst the upper middle classes. Over the next decade the Hills attracted more female volunteers keen to do good things amidst the cultural blockade that prevented them doing anything other than keep house. It was dirty work (and some baulked and gave cash donations instead), but soul salving, rewarding and fashionable. Eventually it reached the aristocracy's top table and, in a manner as radical as Princess Diana's work amongst the land mined and limbless, in November 1876 Queen Victoria's second daughter, the humanitarian and kindly **Princess Alice of Hesse-Darmstadt,** came knocking incognito on the Hill's door asking to be shown round this unknown country of extreme poverty, that zoo of depravation that existed conterminously with the affluent and influential.

As more and more middle- and upper-class female adherents to this peculiar cause came forward, offers to purchase 5 per cent return slum buildings and land pressed in on Octavia and the sisters. Architect Elijah Hoole was employed and Octavia disappeared on a number of trips to Europe and returned with ideas for stylish buildings for the poor of Swiss or German cottage design. Some of these designs incorporated communal rooms, the first ever supervised playgrounds, window boxes, balconies, gardens and features to incorporate beauty into brickwork and sunlight into layout. The still-existing Red Cross Cottages and Hall in Borough (now overhung by the Shard) are an example of Octavia's design ideas for beautification during the 1880s. Tenants and their children were also treated to trips out to the Hill girls' favourite fields, commons and woods, and, as time passed, to properties further away, owned by rich friends or relatives such as step-brother Arthur (see p. 28).

Octavia was quite clear, however, that the tenants for these new improved Ruskin properties, had to be worthy. They would need to be people capable of being spiritually and behaviourally improved, or 'the deal' was off. Thus began the road to multiple (and thereafter fairly continuous) evictions of those tenants judged unsuitable, incorrigible, immoral and undeserving and their replacement with ones Octavia liked, particularly those who paid their rent on time, didn't drink, cared for their homes and generally tolerated her

Red Cross Cottages, hall and gardens, created from the ruins of a fire-damaged paper factory and a pioneering example of a planned relationship between housing, social space and healthful green space. Octavia's friend Henrietta Barnett used such ideas in Hampstead Garden Suburbs and Ebeneezer Howard in Garden Cities.

particular arrangements. Octavia had strong opinions on 'home' and what it should look like and feel like. Much influenced by her grandfather's sanitation reforms she applied her distempering workmen to replace and rectify broken windows, fire risks, leaky gutters, poor water supply, communal sinks and washhouses, as well as blocked drains and cesspits. All these positives were augmented by the process of 'beautification', which some have harshly ruled as the beginnings of modern gentrification processes. Adding beauty allowed Octavia and her sisters to prescribe flowerpots of geraniums and occasionally fresh wildflowers to the blighted dullness of the reality of the working-class poor, whether they wanted them or not. These tenants were probably unconscious of the fact that their rents were paying for it all but in Octavia's view it was better than men spending it on drink, gambling or prostitutes.

The true test of Octavia's system was the weekly check when the rent was collected. This required women volunteers (middle class) knocking on the doors of women (working class) primarily to take in the rent but also having a chat about life matters. It was a cultural bridge that was revolutionary in the era where rent was usually collected by heavies with cudgels and it gave Octavia, her sisters and her female volunteers an insight into a world beyond their understanding.

The visits were kindly and sympathetic in tone, although persistent rent arrears were remedied with evictions, and gradually built into a library of knowledge of individual lives and distressing circumstances. Octavia was shocked that exhausted women with eleven children were not particularly grieved when one or two of their brood died in infancy. It was like a strange menagerie with weekly visits from the keepers to check that the animals hadn't escaped or weren't failing in their duties to perform. It was Octavia's meticulous accountancy and ledgers that drove it along. Alms giving and acts of pecuniary charity were strictly forbidden, as it would only encourage irreligious wastrels, but the books had to be balanced to the nearest penny and **Ruskin** had to get his 5 per cent.

The donations of well-heeled well-wishers provided most of the cash for these experiments in urban housing. The constant theme was the rigid system of rent collecting and recording. The 'work', as Octavia liked to call it, attracted a number of women who preferred the company of other women, like **Emma Cons**. The comments of the poor tenants are not generally recorded. The 'work' also became internationally renowned, attracting **Ellen Chase** from America.

By the mid-1870s the Hill sisters were riding high; after a 20-year association with **Ruskin** and his growing influence, the widening success of the slum housing schemes, the aristocratic and upper class connections forged, the social contacts with the literati and artistic luminaries of the age and the philanthropic support of the wealthy elite, it seemed impossible to fail in any endeavour.

In July 1875, however, that confidence in the future trajectory of better things for all was brought back to earth with a bump. The issue was the intended sale of Swiss Cottage Fields, the fields that Octavia and her sisters had known throughout their childhood and where they had taken their poor tenants and Ragged School children for a taste of the joys of nature and 'the splendours of God's creation'. It was the place that had inspired Octavia's every vision of green and better things in the city slums where she sought so strenuously to add nature's ornamentation. These reminders of the common fields ranged from her tenants' window boxes to their tiny gardens and planted creepers that climbed their walls seeking the wan sunlight. All these additions were just small proxies for the great green spread of Swiss Cottage Fields, its wild flowers that she gathered and the essences of skylarks and butterflies that came with them. It must have come as a shock to realise the fragility of these gifts of nature, childhood joys and genial genie of place in the face of naked commercial desire for land simply as profit, measured in piles of dead, paper money.

Octavia sprang into full campaigning mode, giving a commanding voice to this struggle and pulling in the donations and influence of friends in both high (Hampstead) and low (Marylebone) places as well as the expert legal knowledge of **Robert Hunter** at the

Commons Preservation Society. Although she extracted a promise from the vendor that the land would be sold to her if she raised the requisite amount (£10,000 guineas), which she did, aided by **Edward Bond**, in a very short time, she was cruelly gazumped. The beautiful fields were torn apart by house builders and her common dreamland was traduced and desecrated. Nor was the dismay helped by the black dog mood of her idol **John Ruskin** who, madly grieving after the death of **Rose La Touche** in late May, said, when asked for a donation:

> 'London is utterly doomed – as utterly as Gomorrah. That is no reason why *you* should not open a window or buy a field to give a moment longer breath to her plague-stricken children.'

Notwithstanding Ruskin's gloomy response, Octavia had to cope with suffering her deepest and most impressionable failure. The lessons learned in the battle for Swiss Cottage Fields, however, created the determination to invent a body that could hold land for the benefit of the many, not just the few wealthy enough to own most of the land in the country. It was another history-defining moment, even if it felt like a bitter and crushing defeat.

The loss of Swiss Cottage Fields to the forces of Mammon was traumatic for Octavia. Her faith in all good things, righteousness and trust in people were all challenged at the same time as the visible scars of betrayal were laid out in plots for villas off Fitzjohn's Avenue on the former common fields.

> 'For the moment I am a little broken by the loss, and it would be difficult to begin just at once, to work again.'

Her donors, however, were wealthy enough to suggest that she kept the money and applied it in the general cause of acquiring more open spaces for the benefit of London's poor and downtrodden and she asked herself in 'Space for the People',

> 'whether we cannot find remedies more thorough, and in some measure supply the healing gift of space ... This space it seems is a common gift to man, a thing that he is not specially

Swiss Cottage Fields suffered this fate and spurred the Hills to save London's last commons, create Green Belts and form the National Trust.

bound to provide for himself and his family; where it is not easily inherited it seems to me that it may be given by the state, the city, the millionaire, without danger of destroying the individual's power and habit of energetic self-help ... I think we want four things. Places to sit in, places to play in, places to stroll in, and places to spend a day in.'

Octavia's fourfold geography of open spaces included 'open-air sitting rooms' which stipulated the 'places to sit in' as being

'very near the homes of the poor ... well distributed and abundant.'

After the provision of *supervised* playgrounds ('places to play in'), the obstacle to overcome in the 'places to stroll in' geography was the need to preserve such places as Swiss Cottage Fields within a 1–2 mile walk of people's homes, on the fringes of towns, and to help people use them freely for 'happy outdoor amusement'. Her fourth, 'places to spend a day in' category later became Country Parks, National Parks, Areas of Outstanding Natural Beauty and the estates of the not yet conceived National Trust. It was a remarkable insight into the natural geography of the human condition and another moment of historical importance.

1876 was a busy year for Miranda and Octavia as the Society for the Diffusion of Beauty morphed into the Kyrle Society and its influential sub-committees to whom this message was addressed:

'Men, women, and children want more than food, shelter and warmth. They want, if their lives are to be full and good, space near their homes for exercise, quiet, good air, and sight of grass, trees, and flowers, they want colour, which shall cheer them in the midst of smoke and fog; they want music, which shall contrast with the rattle of motors and lift their hearts to praise and joy; they want suggestion of nobler and better things than those that surround them day by day ... I assure you that I believe these things have more influence on the spirit than we are all accustomed to remember. They cultivate a sense of dignity and self-respect, as well as breaking the monotony of life.'

In her rousing article to stimulate the preservation of London's commons 'Space for the People' in 1875 Octavia concluded with this poetic plea:

'What I wish to urge ... is, the immense value to the education and reformation of our poorest people of some space near their homes, or within reasonable distance of them. We all need space; unless we have it we cannot reach that sense of quiet in which whispers of better things come to us gently. Our lives in London are over-crowded, over-excited, over-strained. This is true of all classes; we all want quiet; we all want beauty for the refreshment of our souls. Sometimes we think of it as a luxury, but when God made the world, He made it very beautiful, and meant that we should live amongst its beauties, and that they should speak peace to us in our daily lives.'

There was not much peace and quiet with **Ruskin** who, in 1877, still deranged with melancholy and obsessing beyond the grave after the death of **Rose La Touche**, flew into a blind rage with Octavia when she made some mild criticism about Ruskin's lack of practicality and refused to pass the slum properties over to his utopian Guild of St. George. This led to a vicious and unwarranted public humiliation through his *Fors Clavigera* that accelerated her nervous breakdown in 1878. Ruskin was not the only reason for this draining of energy and collapse of vigour. There was a peculiar 'one-day engagement' to **Edward Bond** in July 1877 to take into account. Edward lived with his mother, by all accounts a forcefully opinionated woman who had questioned this engagement immediately and forbidden it. Edward, wimpishly, then conveyed this news to his 'fiancée' and Octavia apparently never spoke to him again. She forbade anyone to mention it. Edward died, unmarried, in 1920. Octavia's breakdown required a doctor's prescription of extensive, expensive, foreign holidays with a woman who seems to have mysteriously appeared at the moment of Octavia's greatest vulnerability. Enter the deep-voiced **Harriot Yorke** bearing timetables, trunks and travellers cheques and off they went in January 1878, not once but three times touring around Europe visiting Italy, Switzerland, the Tyrol, France, Greece, Constantinople then up the Danube to Germany. Back in London, sisters Gertrude and Miranda managed all the business affairs during this extended absence until summer 1880, when the prodigal sister and Harriot returned, temporarily 'cured', although Octavia continued to endure health problems for the rest of her life.

Refreshed by the number of trees and bright greenery seen around the houses in Nuremberg, Octavia now commenced the quixotic 'Struggle against Smoke' by inaugurating a new sub-committee of the ever-handy Kyrle Society. To rouse public opinion, scientists, smokeless fuel and smokeless grate manufacturers were dragooned into making a public exhibition of their ideas and practical solutions to the problem at South Kensington. One inventor, Thomas Parker, won a gold medal for the invention of the 'Kyrle grate' and the new fuel 'coalite', which at one time in the 1960s had a plant at Bolsover burning 1 million tons of coal to make smokeless fuel. Merging the economic and ecological views to make her point, Octavia said,

> 'The savings ought to be enormous, the smoke all consists of unconsumed fuel. Some scientific men say that as much as three million out of five million tons used annually flies away in smoke and so does harm and not good. Be the proportion what it may, the waste in fuel is considerable, to say nothing of the cost of the extra washing, and the artificial light required in day-time. But, independently of any question of saving, many of us would, I believe, be ready to make an effort to diminish smoke, were it only for the beauty and comfort and cleanliness, and for the life of the flowers we might then preserve around us.'

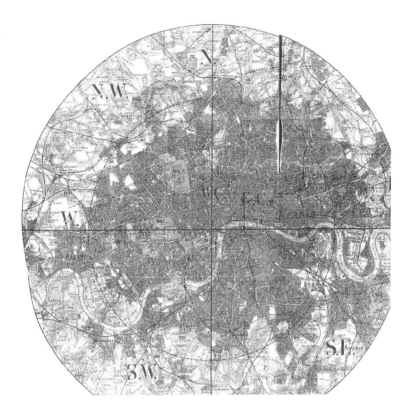

Octavia mapped green spaces and population densities in four quadrants of London to show that there was an eleven-fold difference between the rich West End and the poor East End.

Although Octavia couldn't devote all her energies to this new cause, it lit the spark that spawned the Coal Smoke Abatement Society. The London artist Sir William Blake Richmond inaugurated this society in 1898. He complained that it was too dark to paint in winter due to the smoke. He likened the darkness to a total eclipse of the sun. Visible air pollution was eventually tackled after the lethal London smogs in the 1950s, but today's invisible but no less lethal air pollution is still causing 23,000 unnecessary deaths annually in Britain. The announcement in 2017 that all new petrol and diesel cars will be phased out by 2040 seems to miss the point that by then nearly half a million unnecessary deaths will have occurred. *Plus ça change* …

In 1888 Octavia was pursuing the theme of 'More Air for London' with great vigour, animated by some scientific research that would have pleased her maternal grandfather. It deployed, as he had done, the drawing of circles of four- and six-mile radii from Charing Cross on a Stanford map. These circles were then quartered and in each quarter all the built areas and green spaces of the city were measured. Having determined the number of these areas Octavia then cross-matched the populations that would have access to the open spaces. The results were completely conclusive and dramatic. In the rich West End there was eleven times as much space as there was in the poor East End. Even more dramatic was the statistic that each acre in the affluent West End was shared by 682 people, but in the poverty-stricken East End 7,481 people had to share that space.

In her paper, which included the first use of the term 'Green Belt', Octavia lamented the lack of urban fringe field paths surrounded by open space where people could walk out from the cities and towns, breathe fresh air, and let their children run and take healthy exercise away from the smoke and grime of the urban slums. Her strategy was to acquire a ring of commons, hills and open spaces connected by paths around the urban boundary of London so that everyone could enjoy

'the life-enhancing virtues of pure earth, clean air and blue sky.'

She was helped by **Robert Hunter**, Solicitor to the Commons Preservation Society. By 1884 Robert bore the scars of spending nearly 20 years fighting a David and Goliath battle against the forces of unchristian greed and self-interest in the cause of common land preservation for the benefit of his fellow citizens. These contests for the Commons Preservation Society were legal struggles demanding near-impossible discoveries and proofs of faded rights of common, or putting up witnesses too poor to defend themselves or frightened off by threats of violence or destitution. In defending the poor commoners of Epping Forest, the son of one of the commoners, called Willingale, protesting about the illegal fencing of the common by the very unchristian Reverend Maitland, had been thrown in jail where he caught pneumonia and died. The weakness of the law was apparent – if all the commoners failed to attend court or they died, then there was no locus to form a case to defend their rights and the common itself would be lost for ever. **Robert Hunter** was as much motivated by these legal injustices as was Octavia Hill by housing squalor and lack of urban open spaces. His canvas was different and required a detailed legal argument for each and every case brought to court, where expenses were also an enormous additional concern and often used as part of the bullying tactics of injustice.

Conscious of these limitations, Hunter sought to formulate a general case for a body capable of receiving gifts of rights of common, or manorial rights, or the commons themselves on behalf of the public. In September 1884, when **George John Shaw-Lefevre** was President of the National Association for the Promotion of Social Science, Hunter took the opportunity of taking a paper entitled: 'A Suggestion for the Better Preservation of Open Spaces' to its annual conference in Birmingham to describe his idea. A vital thread in the National Trust story started with this speech. When Octavia called for a 'Commons and Gardens Trust' she reflected the essence of Hunter's paper, which in turn was distilled, in part, from her own actions. At the start of the paper he laid out the case for action derived from the calamitous impacts of the Enclosure Acts during the past forty years:

'Between six and seven hundred thousand acres were reduced to private ownership and many square miles of country were deprived of every fragment of open land, save where a driftway was left by a road side, or an acre or two spared for a Recreation Ground. At length London took alarm. Her population was increasing by gigantic strides. Leafy suburbs were rapidly being converted into treeless wastes of houses, and fields and hedgerows were vanishing before the builder in every direction.'

Hunter then proposed a 'remedy for the defects' of the situation:

'I advocate the formation of a Corporate Company ... the main functions of this Company would consist of;
(1) The acquisition and holding of properties to which common rights are attached
(2) The acquisition of manors, manorial rights and wastes of manors, downs, moors and other open spaces
(3) The acquisition of square gardens, disused churchyards and burial grounds and any other spaces suitable for town gardens ...'

Hunter said at the paper's conclusion,

'The central idea is that of a Land Company, formed, not for the promotion of thrift or the spread of political principles, and not primarily for profit, but with a view to the protection of the public interests in the open spaces of the country. An experience of nearly twenty years in defending open spaces has convinced me that an organisation such as I have suggested would cure a radical defect in the existing machinery for the purpose, and would supply a most valuable means by which to give effect to public opinion on the subject of open spaces.'

The paper prescribed maintaining these spaces 'in their natural condition' and as 'places of resort for recreation and instruction'. These features passed down into much of the mid-20th century legislation that created National Nature Reserves, National Parks and Areas of Outstanding Natural Beauty. It is easy, with this knowledge, to see also how this 'Land Company' for saving commons and town gardens for recreation and nature morphed into the 'big idea' for the National Trust and how the earlier, seemingly quaint, ideas and actions of the Kyrle Society, the Hill sisters and his own sister Dorothy influenced **Robert Hunter**. Even more bizarrely, when supporters of his idea in the Commons Preservation Society had the speech published it was circulated in the USA. This then influenced the setting up of American preservationist 'Land Companies' as Trusts in Massachusetts in 1891, which Hunter then borrowed back to form the constitution of the fledgling National Trust in 1894.

Hunter, as a young lawyer, had been battling in and out of courts to save threatened commons in and around London since 1865 when **George John Shaw-Lefevre**, philosopher John Stuart Mill and a host of other influential gentlemen founded the radical Commons Preservation Society. It had obtained Parliamentary action to create Commons Acts to stop the enclosure of commons and for managing them better. By 1884 it had won brilliant victories to save Hampstead Heath, Wimbledon Common and Wandsworth Common and was finishing off the task of saving the vast woodland common that was Epping Forest. **Robert Hunter** had also worked with Octavia and Miranda Hill to protect Burnham Beeches, Vauxhall Park and Parliament Hill for the Open Spaces Committee of the Kyrle Society. A new challenge emerged in 1883 when the relatives of John Evelyn approached Octavia to acquire and protect his home and gardens at Sayes Court, Deptford (which Hunter mentioned anonymously in his speech). This had followed, and was possibly a direct result of, a public lambasting of London's wealthy by Octavia during the bid to save Parliament Hill.

> 'I cannot but think in the Metropolis where rates press heavily on the poor there should be so many a rich and generous-hearted man who would like to contribute something above his share of the rate to give his fellow townsmen some few acres of sloping ground with shady trees ... I should like myself nothing better, if I had the money, than to make so great and lasting gift to the public.'

The problem with Sayes Court was not that it needed money, because a generous-hearted family had already offered to gift it to the public. The difficulty, as identified in **Robert Hunter**'s 1884 paper, was that there was no simple legal body, his 'Land Company', that could receive such gifts on behalf of the people. Both Robert and Octavia were determined to create such a body although Octavia expressed the view that

'People don't like unsuccessful business, but do like charity when a little money goes a long way because of good commercial management.'

In this now well-known exchange of letters in 1885, she wrote that it needed a 'short and expressive name', adding to her letter to Hunter,

'What do you think of the Commons and Gardens Trust?'

– with the often-unmentioned but very specific subscript,

'for accepting, holding, preserving and purchasing open spaces for the people in town and country.'

Octavia thought that the word 'Trust' conveyed a better sense of public benevolence than the commercial tone implicit in the word 'company' that Hunter had suggested in 1884. Hunter then famously scribbled the words

'? National Trust'.

Although this was the first mention of the National Trust as a brand name, the signposts to it had started decades before. The thread had been drawn together by Miranda and Octavia's desires for green belts, slum gardens, burial grounds as open-air sitting rooms, window boxes and even bunches of wild flowers to brighten the lives of the poor. It was a product of inner city environmental degradation and social injustice (coupled with the knowledge that on the fringes of every town there were sunshine, fresh air and greenery) as much as it was a utilisation of **Robert Hunter**'s skill as a lawyer in the saving of that larger and more ancient folk space, the common. The idea was the same, the creation or retention of 'soul' space for the people. It was a counter-revolution to the prevailing culture of land-grab and greed that had already reduced the vast rural commons and communal space for the agricultural population.

The poetry of **John Clare** recorded some of the revulsion and distaste that this ethos created in the defenceless rural reality of much of England. It met its match when the land-grabbing tidal wave washed against the back gardens of London lawyers. The total acreage of common land had fallen by millions of acres over the preceding few centuries of enclosure and resulted in the dispersal of English peasantry to the new industrial towns, where they were crammed in eight to a room. These conditions first awakened the good Christian anguish of the reformist Octavia Hill.

Even though it was the beginning of a brand it was also the end for Sayes Court, which couldn't be saved. It was a whole decade later before the National Trust was incorporated; this was not ten years of idleness but of organisation and overcoming obstacles. Indeed, in 1885, there was a trial run with leaflets printed for an 'Open Spaces Preservation and Land Development Society' suggesting that subscribers might purchase £20,000-worth of £1 shares to fund a company something like the Kyrle Society. The concept bombed for unknown reasons.

Meanwhile in the peaceful, poetic grandeur of the Lake District the locals were revolting. Some 'locals', however, were recently arrived, ex-Oxford University residents like **John Ruskin** and **Hardwicke Drummond Rawnsley** and the cause of the revolt was the spreading metal tentacles of the manic railway monster. Ruskin had a deep pathological hatred of railways and when the Monsal Dale line skewered the Wye valley of the Peak District in the 1860s he ranted,

'The valley is gone, and the Gods with it; and now, every fool in Buxton can be in Bakewell in half an hour, and every fool in Bakewell in Buxton; which you think a lucrative process of exchange – you Fools everywhere.'

The threat to desecrate the 'sacred ground' of Wordsworth with railways from Keswick to Buttermere and up the Honister Pass in 1883 erupted with a volcanic fury of words that nicely reflected the geological processes that created the Lake District and the slate the railway was seeking to extract. Out of this rage sprang the Rawnsley-inspired Lake District Defence Society, although most of its members lived in London. They included poets and writers Alfred Tennyson, Matthew Arnold and **Robert Browning** as well as landowning magnate the Duke of Westminster, the Kyrle Society President.

After seeing off a railway to Ennerdale, the closure threat to footpaths alongside Derwentwater and over Latrigg came to **Rawnsley**'s attention. In September 1887 Rawnsley's associate, Henry Jenkinson, stormed the castle by bringing 500 or so protestors to the doorstep of one of the landowners, and Rawnsley held awareness-raising protest meetings in large cities. The society organised an unblocking, mass trespass, party of 2000 walkers including **Samuel Plimsoll** (he of the line, and later the shoes) to assert the public right. The landowner of Latrigg, Mrs Spedding, issued a writ for damages but a court compromise confirmed most of the rights of access and other blocking landowners gave in.

Throughout the 1880s there was an ongoing debate between the Commons Preservation Society and the Kyrle Society's Open Spaces Committee about whether to put greater weight on tempting the state to take action to preserve open spaces, footpaths, places of beauty and historic interest through legislation or to do it themselves. The Commons Preservation Society (chaired by **John George Shaw-Lefevre**) had been buoyed by the initial success of the Ancient Monuments Protection Act in saving some prehistoric places and maybe thought that a wider obligation on the state would avoid the need for a voluntary land-holding body – a cause which might perhaps draw resources of cash away from the legal costs of fighting cases in the courts or lobbying Parliament. In 1889 he had sent Octavia a negative opinion when approached as a potential leader of the putative Trust.

It was the potential loss, in 1893, of the Lodore Falls and the island that makes Grasmere so picturesque, however, that finally pulled the legal trigger. It was also the 'bing, bang, bosh' element of Rawnsley's character that the nascent National Trust needed, and because the Lake District held a special affection for Octavia, with its associations with **Ruskin** and her long-time friend Mary Harris, delay was not an option. Rawnsley, Hunter and Hill met at the home of the Duke of Westminster to nail it. On 16 November 1893 the first meeting was held, where Rawnsley roused the audience with the suggestion that they were creating 'a great National Gallery of natural pictures', followed by a formal proposal and seconding at Grosvenor House on 16 July 1894. The National Trust was now deemed to be the 'general trustee for all property intended for the use and enjoyment of the nation at large'. On 12 December the Memorandum and Articles of Association were witnessed and by 12 January 1895 registered with the Board of Trade. History was being made.

The final phase of the construction of the framework for the National Trust had occupied the whole of 1894, with **Robert Hunter** doing most of the legal drafting. Some of this was borrowed from the white Americans, who were busily defining their own framework over the landscapes of the dispossessed Native Americans with public benefactions of recreational reservation land. Although the views of national emparkers like John Muir, Frederick Law Olmsted and Henry David Thoreau differed by degrees of wildness and public accessibility, the basic principle of creating a new nation by denying and denigrating the previous Native American managers of the land, as shown by Professor Ken Olwig, clearly smacks of racism as well as, in some places like Yosemite, ecological folly by failing to regularly burn the scrub and coarse grasses. The new Americans' concept of creating parks *for ever* was not necessarily consistent with parks *for everyone*. Nevertheless, Octavia's contacts with **Ellen Chase** enabled **Robert Hunter** to receive copies of the documents related to the 1891 Massachusetts Trust for Public Reservations.

In Wales, one of **John Ruskin**'s former associates, Fanny Talbot, was prepared to encourage other donors by giving a piece of cliff, Dinas Oleu near Barmouth, the 'fortress of light' (provided that the Trust did not put in any of those abominable 'cast iron seats of serpentine design'). James Potter (father of Beatrix) stumped up to be the Trust's first life member. **William Morris**'s Society for the Preservation of Ancient Buildings was alert with ideas to save medieval buildings from the culture of 'scrape' or feckless restoration by removing plaster from church walls. The society suggested Long Crendon Court House and Alfriston Clergy House as potential acquisitions. Wicken Fen, Cambridgeshire, was acquired in 1899 in the Fenland – where only 0.01 per cent of the area is now fen.

Octavia was greatly delighted with the acquisition of the coastal open space land at Barras Head around Tintagel and was moved to write of its success as an early 'crowd-funded' venture:

> 'It is not quite the first, nor will it, I hope, be the last of such places which shall thus become in a new and very real sense the Common Land of England. But it is the very first which has been not given by one far-sighted and generous donor, but purchased by the combined help of many – rich and poor, near and far, American and English – giving each in their measure to buy a bit of England as the common playground, study, resting place, vantage ground for seeing the holy things of nature.'

Inevitably there was some purposeful clustering of new acquisitions around the country homes of the co-creators: Brandlehow in Rawnsley's Lake District; One Tree Hill, Ide Hill, Toys Hill, Mariners Hill and Crockham Hill in Kent near 'Larksfield', the house, that **Harriot Yorke** built for herself and Octavia to escape London after the Nottingham Place School closed in 1884; and Waggoners Wells, Hindhead and the Devil's Punchbowl near **Robert Hunter**'s home at Haslemere, Surrey.

In 1904 Barrington Court, Somerset, was acquired and both Octavia and Harriot were not amused (Harriot had threatened to resign as Treasurer in 1898 if any more houses were bought). The aims being set out in practice were, instead, to buy or acquire a 'green belt' of open spaces and connecting footpaths like a green string of pearls around any town, city or village. None of the National Trust appeals for open space failed whilst Octavia and Harriot were alive.

However, as with the American parks, Octavia's concept might have been to acquire land for *ever* but it was not intended for *everyone,* as she declared that the Trust

> 'by no means plan to give access to the tramp, the London rough, the noisy beanfeaster, or the shouting crowds of

children … but plan to preserve the land in its natural state for the artist, the professional man, and such of the public as appreciate and respect natural beauty.'

Octavia never had a formal position in the National Trust but was very alive to appeals and to Sir **Robert Hunter**'s framing of the National Trust Act 1907, which gave it the amazing statutory power of declaring its land inalienable to compulsory purchase without special parliamentary procedures. By the time of Octavia's death in 1912, The National Trust still only had 500–700 members and by 1919 owned just 63 small properties covering around 6000 acres.

Among her many other ideas and achievements during her lifetime were Army Cadets and supervised playgrounds. The Southwark Army Cadet Company was created in 1889 by Octavia Hill anxious that poor boys from her housing projects should not descend into lives of indolence or crime. As she had observed in her playgrounds, boys required discipline to avoid disruptive chaos. She persuaded contacts at Eton College to pay for bright red uniforms to make the cadets stand out on the parade ground.

"There is no organisation which I found that influences the boys so powerfully for good as that of our cadets."

The militaristic aspect of the Cadets was not to everyone's taste, however, and her pacifist acquaintances did not approve. The Cadets morphed into the Army Cadet Force in 1942, admitted girls in the 1980s and now has about 40,000 members. She also became a Poor Law Commissioner in 1905, appointed alongside George Lansbury, Beatrice Webb and Charles Boothby.

Touchingly, Octavia arranged for Elijah Hoole, her architect, to design a gravestone for Miranda, herself and Harriot and for all to be buried in the same grave beneath the whispering yew trees in the quiet of Crockham churchyard. In doing so she turned down the chance to be buried with other national heroes in Westminster Abbey.

EMILY SOUTHWOOD HILL, 'Millie', 1840–1931 (eleventh sibling)
Emily was born in September 1840 in Loughton, Essex and died in September 1931 aged 91 at Eirene Cottage, Hampstead, London. She enjoyed the wild country-girl life as well as sharing the urban duties whenever Octavia collapsed; she took on the **F D Maurice** Scholarship at Queen's College to add to the family income and acquire teaching qualifications. In her early years Millie once overbalanced and fell headfirst into a waterbutt whilst playing at sailing half walnut shells and was rescued from drowning by the quick-thinking Octavia pushing the butt over. These were supportive sisters. It developed further when Octavia handed over the property management work to her and **Emma Cons**. In 1878 Millie responded again by taking on the administration of the Kyrle Society donations fund when Octavia's health crisis required the trip to Europe with **Harriot Yorke**.

Emily married **Charles Edmund Maurice** (the son of F D Maurice) on 29 August 1872 at Christ Church, Marylebone, London. They worked together to edit the vast collection of Octavia's correspondence after her death with the intention of publishing a glorious testimony to her elder sister's life and work. As with all such projects, unless handled by an archivist the editing can over simplify, with the focus on heroic success at the expense of the real person. It is thought that a degree of moral censorship may have gone on and their editing might have resulted in destruction of material they didn't approve of. We will never know.

In later years Emily was active in the planning for Hampstead Garden Suburb with the Barnetts and others.

FLORENCE HILL, 'Florrie', 1843–1935 (twelfth sibling)
Florence was born in Leeds on 5 September 1843 and died unmarried in October 1935 in Stepney Green. The youngest of the sisters, she was somewhat in awe of her elder siblings' all-knowing powers and once, as a child, asked Octavia when playing with a local mutt,

'Ockey, is that dog happy?'

She received the outdoor instruction that all the others received but had the benefit of her sisters' intimate knowledge of their own special places. They were known locally in Finchley as 'the young ladies who are always up in the hedges'. It was a carefree, blissful time of exploration and adventure. As one observer said of the girls,

> 'They knew every boy and girl, cat, dog and donkey in the village by sight, and a good many of them by name, and for those whose names they do not know they invent one.'

For health reasons it was decided in 1855 that Florrie should go to live with her aunt Emily Southwood Smith in Florence, Italy. She became fluent in Italian and good at music and the location attracted other sisters on visits to their aunt including Miranda, and Octavia, who overwintered there in 1867 during the excitements caused by Garibaldi and Italian reunification. Florence was invited to Darmstadt by Queen Victoria's daughter **Princess Alice** to organise a similar social housing scheme to Octavia's when she became Grand Duchess of Hesse. Once back in England in 1894 Florence's health dictated a move out of dirty, noisy London with her mother to Tunbridge Wells, although she occasionally holidayed in Transylvania. Whatever she did for her health it seemed to have worked and she lived until 92.

Florence lived simply and devoted herself to the poorest of the poor in the East End of London. Although she owned a comfortable house in Hampstead and had inherited Octavia's cottage at Toys Hill, she spent 30 years from 1905 to her death working as a Sunday school teacher for the local Unitarian Chapel and living in a tiny house in the East End.

The whispering continues:
how the Hill family changed our world

Social housing management

Octavia Hill was against handouts to the poor, school dinners, free health care and old age pensions lest people become over-dependent on others. Her focus was on 'a hand up not a handout' She was also against suffragettes because she believed 'women were unsuited to thinking about the big issues of finance and foreign policy'. She wanted the 'deserving poor' to self-improve through work and moral education. As her managed slum tenant estates grew after her deals with the Ecclesiastical Commissioners in the 1880s, interested local authorities also began to operate their own schemes, which soon outnumbered hers. Octavia saw these council estates as unconnected to the tenants and not conducive to the doorstep self-improvement negotiations that took place under her personal visitor-led approach. Her ideas became unfashionable and expensive when paid professional staff replaced the volunteers and only a few Octavia-inspired housing schemes now remain.

One wonders what Octavia Hill would have made of the dreadful Grenfell Tower flammable cladding inferno of 15 June 2017, and its appalling loss of life, where the social housing tenants had been reporting their worries about the building to the local authority for some time. Octavia *listened* to her tenants, *repaired* their buildings and religiously *improved* the basic conditions of their lives, including finding them work opportunities. She was criticised by **William Morris**, who said that despite such improvements it simply wasn't morally right to cram a family of eight into a single room, but she persevered in *listening* to people, 'her people'.

The Royal Borough of Kensington and Chelsea contains not only some of the most affluent parts of the UK but also some of the poorest. The Grenfell Tower disaster was in the poorest part and affected the poorest people; it is now a police crime scene. A public inquiry may (or may not) reveal the complex truth. However, the simpler truths about how the poor are treated now have a new expression and link us through the intervening 150 years to Octavia Hill's time as a slum-improving landlord.

The National Trust

The National Trust co-founded by Octavia Hill in 1895 is not the institution that operates today. First, it has far exceeded its founders', or anyone else's, expectations at its early beginnings. The National Trust is arguably the world's best multiple-purpose land manager. Its land holdings cover 630,000 acres (247,000 hectares) and contain some of the most iconic landscapes, nature and buildings of England, Wales and Northern Ireland. However, the co-founders' ideals, and Octavia's sisters' promptings, concerning making scraps of land available to poor people for air and exercise close to where they live and for enjoying 'the beauty of God's handiwork' have been somewhat eclipsed over a century of increased building acquisitions. The vast majority of the acres of the Trust's rural property portfolio is now far, far away from the lives of the approximately 90 per cent of the population who inhabit cities or towns or those without access to a car, or the financial means to get there to enjoy it. Is the idealism that prompted the passion to attempt to save Swiss Cottage Fields from housing development for those desperate poor of the urban hellholes still visible? Is the fire that burned within to secure the last of London's urban-fringe commons from developers still alight? Who within the Trust keeps this beautiful social equity campaigning flame alive today?

The National Trust has recently announced its intention to spend £100 million of its supporters' money every year for ten years on repairing its stock of around 300 grand houses, coast and countryside, but very little on land acquisition in the places close to where the vast majority of people live and could most benefit from natural beauty of any description. The question that might be asked by

Octavia Hill, if she were alive today, is why, given the strict protocols of endowments called 'the Chorley formula', are these stately homes not all paying their way? Partly it is because many properties were donated before the Trust established an endowment protocol and it is now saddled with financial liabilities that are very difficult to overcome. Octavia was always wary of the liabilities inherent in the Trust's building acquisitions and **Harriot Yorke**, who sat on the Trust's major committees after Octavia had died, was even more scathing. Octavia had very strict rules for her slum housing tenants who could not pay their way and evicted them without hesitation. The question that might be asked now is, should the National Trust re-order its housing estate?

Should it lose a few of its expensive-to-maintain but not inalienable country houses that don't pay their way, as the Youth Hostel Association has been forced to do with some of its buildings, and sell them off as investment properties? Should it take a leaf out of the book of similar heritage building preservation bodies like the Landmark Trust that recoup their costs through holiday lettings, so that many more portions of their grand buildings are constantly used by enthusiastic visitors *and* pay their way? The Landmark Trust owns some large mansions in addition to the stock of fine vernacular holiday cottages, so size does not seem to be an issue.

The National Trust has always described itself as an evolving body, and has conducted many reviews of its constitutional arrangements ever since it was formed, beginning with its own Act of Parliament in 1907. That review gave it exceptional powers of inalienability so that it could not be forced to release its property to state interests unless both Houses of Parliament agreed. It has suffered inertia but it has also listened to challenges and undertaken changes. It may soon have six million subscribing members, most of them living in urban and suburban settings. Should the Trust not now ask itself the pertinent marketing question, what is its urban and urban fringe offer? What will its next million urban members expect for their subscriptions – something naturally beautiful on their doorsteps, perhaps, and the opportunity to engage in creating new history close to where the majority 'live, work and raise their families'?

The National Trust, to its credit, however, has been working with Birmingham City Council and the Canals and Rivers Trust on the Roundhouse Project. It has also embarked recently on a mini-crusade funded by £230,000 of Heritage Lottery Fund money to help financially parched local authorities like Newcastle City Council create a future-proofed, independent land trust to keep the city's stock of urban parks secure from loss. This is not a miniaturised version of the National Trust in the urban North East, but it allows the Newcastle City Council to utilise the Trust's expertise in trustee land management and decide if it wants to transfer its land to another body. Sheffield City Council considered such a deal with the National Trust to create an independent trust but turned it down; there were reasons of a political nature. Other Northern cities might be similarly attracted to this new concept as 'austerity' measures cut deeply into parks and open space maintenance budgets. The big question seems to be, is this enough to satisfy the Trust's urban members and future members, or is something more demonstrative needed in the Green Belts and urban fringe lands that surrounds them?

Green Belts

Green Belts, a concept created by Octavia Hill following her childhood playing in urban fringe meadows and green fields enjoying the simple beauties of nature, are under immediate threat. The threat now is as clear and apparent as it was in the late 19th century when the precious green space of Swiss Cottage Fields, used by hundreds of people for healthy open-air recreation, was acquired by housing developers. Even after Octavia Hill and her benefactors had raised the money to buy the land for public use, the developers reneged on the deal and carried on regardless. This was the harsh lesson that created the need to form a corporate body that could legally hold land 'for everyone, for ever', as the Commons Preservation Society could not, at that time, provide that service. That body is the National Trust. There is now a need for leadership and a coalition of landowning conservation bodies in the fight to save the Green Belts and the rural urban fringes of towns and cities everywhere, for the public good, for ever. The very places where the Hill sisters saw and defined natural beauty in the simple blades of grass and common wildflowers, the space being used for children's play and for adults to breathe and admire the setting sun, are still being bullied and bulldozed. Successive recent governments have *spoken* loftily of preserving the 14 Green Belts in England but then done exactly the opposite by making house-building a priority and changing the rules of the planning system. The truth, which Octavia learned with the wanton destruction of Swiss Cottage Fields, is that where human greed is concerned, nothing is sacred.

There is surely a more responsible way of measuring and valuing this land for the multiple public benefits that it provides. Natural capital evaluation evidence has shown that the *annual* value of London's formal parks alone is a staggering £92 billion, mainly because of the health and wellbeing benefits they provide – those that the Hill sisters instinctively recognised. They probably thought of them as priceless. The annual value of the benefits of the Metropolitan Green Belt has yet to be assessed but will undoubtedly be many £billions more, especially if its degraded agricultural landscapes are repaired first. Professor Dieter Helm, Chairman of the government's Natural Capital Committee, has argued cogently that the Green Belts should not be built over, as there is no viable compensatory land to accommodate their loss, a key principle of natural capital economics. They need their original purpose to be upheld, and better permanent protection.

New commons

Octavia joined the Commons Preservation Society to help in the fight to save the last of the London commons from housing developers. The society led the legal crusade for the preservation of commons and common rights in a variety of Acts of Parliament from the Metropolitan Commons Act 1866 through to the Commons Act 2006. Throughout this 140-year period the 'golden thread' to create new rights of common has remained unbroken in law. This is an important matter because it is clear that it is the will of Parliament for commons to evolve through time, reflecting society's relationship with land. As Professor Chris Rodgers has found in a recent study, registration of a new common can, now, only be achieved by a landowner *voluntarily* granting rights of common. Registration cannot be acquired by long use or 'prescription' as in the ancient past. The creation of a new common occurred once in the 20th century when Daphne Buxton, a benevolent Norfolk landowner, determinedly created the new Rushall Common by granting a right of common of *'estovers'* to a local resident over a plot of land she owned. The main rights of common that can be given by grant are *grazing* (cattle, sheep, horses, geese, etc.); *pannage* (pigs foraging for acorns and beech mast); *turbary* (peat or turf for fuel); *piscary* (fish); *common in soil* (soil, gravel, stone); *estovers* (fallen wood, sticks, bracken) and *fructus naturales* (wild herbs, fungi, berries, fruits, etc.). These were all derived from activities necessary to life for medieval peasants and in many instances the loss of common rights during the prolonged period of enclosures by the powerful lords of the manor meant the difference between life and death. Enclosure was certainly the death of a self-sustaining lifestyle for millions of English peasants. Their displacement represented the English 'clearances' refined with such devastating effect in the Scottish Highlands.

New commons, such as the one proposed by the Land Trust in the Dearne Valley Nature Improvement Area, could cover tracts of the Green Belts or the rural-urban fringes and also, when registered, give the public access for 'air and exercise' close to where people live, thus fulfilling Octavia's dreams. The scope for new commons creation is vast: benevolent landowners, local authorities, public health bodies, developers and builders, kindly farmers and forest or woodland owners could all make a permanent difference to the lives of millions and they would not even need to dispose of their land, simply change rights over its use.

Access to land

The mid-20th century saw the establishment of planning laws (including Green Belts), National Parks, Areas of Outstanding Natural Beauty, Long Distance Paths and Public Rights of Way, together attending to most of the items on the Hill sisters 'to do' list. Later came Heritage Coasts and Country Parks and access to mountains, moors, heaths, downs and commons (the 'right to roam') at the turn of the 21st century, with the completion of the England (and Wales) Coast Path the latest priority task.

New evidence of public use of the landscape, however, has shown that we do not stray very far from 'home'. This research (Monitor of Engagement with the Natural Environment) has created greater awareness of the fact that only about half of the population ever visit the natural environment of green places. Of those that actually get outside into the open air the vast majority do not go much further than one to two miles from where they live. As around 90 per cent of the population live in cities, urban extensions, large towns and rural towns, this makes the parks, green spaces, public rights of way and Green Belt within and immediately around the urban boundary the most critical places to ensure a host of benefits including the most basic of all – human health and mental wellbeing. Much of the current activity in this zone is conducted by walkers and particularly those walking dogs. However, its potential as a place for active recreation, thus tackling some aspects of the obesity and mental health crises, as well as its potential contribution to climate change adaptation by the planting of more deciduous forests, has yet to be turned into policy and practice. It seems it is mainly the middle classes that venture much beyond five miles from home to visit the remote and more spectacular places that Britain offers, but even then this is only a small proportion (about 10 per cent) of the population.

Octavia was motivated by the destruction of Swiss Cottage Fields by housing developers. In the 1960s when it became clear to the National Trust that the entire English and Welsh coastal edge was at risk from similarly disfiguring development, it took action and Operation Neptune was conceived. It began a campaign to buy or otherwise acquire by gift or donation as much coastal landscape as possible to preserve this precious 'edge' environment so that as many people as possible could enjoy it for ever and as much wildlife as possible could find refuge. It was a hugely successful campaign and visitors and locals alike enjoy its fruits each year. Perhaps now would be a good time to launch a similar campaign for the urban fringe and Green Belts? It could be called Operation Octavia in her honour.

Such a campaign could showcase the potential for adding beauty to the 'edge' environment at the border between the built and the un-built. The acquisition or gifts of land around every settlement would remedy the defect of open space deficit and, particularly for children, would offer the future associations with nature that switch on a lifelong affinity of caring for the environment – a place that we all ultimately depend upon for our sustenance and spiritual enjoyment. This campaign of acquisitions could immortalise the desire of Octavia Hill and her siblings to provide space for the people close to where they live in a way that has been perpetually thwarted since the loss of Swiss Cottage Fields. It might require an alliance of land-holding bodies to mastermind an appeal for gifts of land and donations to provide an endowment for their maintenance, or it could operate through some form of specifically conceived new trust. Something should be done and now is the time to do it.

The 'whispers' need urgent amplification and the 'better things' require action; we all need the 'healing gift of space'. Perhaps we should leave the last word to Octavia Hill to speak for all her family and indeed for all of us.

> 'The need of quiet, the need of air, the need of exercise: the sight of sky and of things growing seem human needs, common to all.'

Hill family influences

HANS CHRISTIAN ANDERSEN (2 April 1805 – 4 August 1875)
The great Danish fairy-story writer met the young Hill sisters when visiting Mary Howitt, his Danish–English book translator. The Hill sisters thought he might like to play and took him to the annual Highgate haymaking at their Hillside house. HCA seems not to have contributed much and the girls grew bored with his silence and wandered off to entertain themselves, leaving the great Dane to irritably seek sulky indoor solace.

PRINCESS LOUISE CAROLINE ALBERTA, DUCHESS OF ARGYLE
(18 March 1848 – 3 December 1939)
Princess Louise became a supporter of the Kyrle Society's initiatives and opened Vauxhall Park with her husband in 1890. Following the creation of the National Trust she also opened Brandlehow in the Lake District in 1902 and took on the role of royal patronage as the Trust's President. Her personal life was fairly exotic for a daughter of Queen Victoria. She liked to be called 'Mrs Campbell' on incognito walkabouts; and there were allegations of an affair with the sculptor Joseph Boehm, who died in her arms in his London studio.

CHARLES ROBERT ASHBEE (17 May 1863 – 23 May 1942)
An Arts and Crafts architect and a secret homosexual who enjoyed a marriage of convenience with wealthy and impetuous Janet Forbes, which resulted in four children. He started an East End Guild of Arts and Crafts in the Toynbee Hall settlement to train poor cockney boys in furniture and design. Ashbee fell out with Octavia Hill over the use of one of the National Trust's first properties, Long Crendon Courthouse, that he was engaged to repair whilst also using it as a place for poor children to enjoy the countryside and engage in artistic enterprise. He wanted to move in Guild furniture and have its sign over the door, but Octavia strongly disagreed and ensured that she got her way. Ashbee in letters to his wife Janet called Octavia 'the lady in the mushroom hat' (and probably a few other things). The Ashbees moved on to other eclectic projects and adulterous events.

HENRIETTA BARNETT (4 May 1851–10 June 1936)

'Yetta', formerly Henrietta Rowland (Macassar oil heiress), met the Hills shortly after moving to Bayswater in 1869 and became one of Octavia's best early friends and one of her keenest volunteers. She married fellow Christian Socialist Rev. **Samuel Barnett** in 1873, shortly after which he became vicar of St Jude's, the worst slum parish in Whitechapel and inhabited by around 2000 prostitutes. As a result she and Jane Senior created the Metropolitan Association for Befriending Young Servants, aimed at preventing girls from drifting into vice and alcoholism. Knowing that slum children never saw the countryside or the sea she formed the Children's Fresh Air Mission (1877) and later, the Children's Country Holiday Fund and the Homes for Workhouse Girls (1880). She was also a pioneering female town planner inspired by Ebenezer Howard; Hampstead Garden Suburb designer with architects Unwin and Lutyens; co-instigator of Toynbee Hall 'University Settlement' in 1884; member of the National Union of Women Workers; founder of the Whitechapel Art Gallery; and was active in the Workers' Educational Association with William Beveridge and Clement Attlee.

The Barnetts changed with the times but they felt Octavia became more dogmatic and jingoistic in her keen support of the war with the Boers and the role her Southwark army cadets, trained by General Maurice, might play. Octavia had invented 'army cadets' as a result of her observations of boisterous boys in her children's playgrounds, where she quickly saw the need for stern adult supervision.

Samuel became a Canon *c.* 1893 and Henrietta a Dame in 1924. Her epitaph to Octavia balanced the good and bad aspects of Octavia's character:

> 'She was strong-willed, some thought self-willed, but the strong will was never for self. She was impatient in little things, persistent with long-suffering in big ones; often dictatorial in manner but humble to self-effacement before those she loved or admired. She had high standards for everyone, for herself ruthlessly exalted ones, and she dealt out disapprobation and often scorn to those who fell below her standards for them,

but she somewhat erred in sympathy by urging them to attain her standards for them, instead of their own for themselves.'

JEREMY BENTHAM (15 February 1748–6 June 1832)
A utilitarian philosopher, influencer of **Robert Owen** and John Stuart Mill and friend of Dr Thomas Southwood Smith. Bentham volunteered his cadaver to be used for medical research and was the first human body to be preserved for public display as an anatomical specimen. Although the Anatomy Act legalising the use of unclaimed bodies had not yet been passed, Bentham had noticed Thomas's work and he requested that Dr Southwood Smith use his body after death for the world's first public dissection. This duly took place in a crowded rotunda with a circular roof light eerily illuminated by lightning during a loud thunderstorm on 9 June 1832. It had been intended that his head would be stuffed, but a Maori-inspired process involving sulphuric acid failed to look attractive and a wax face with some real hair was used instead. His auto-icon remains are still at University College London, albeit in a locked cabinet.

EDWARD BOND (October 1844–18 August 1920)
Edward was alleged to have become 'engaged' to Octavia in July 1877. It was public news for just one day. Whether this was intended to be a 'marriage of convenience' or one of genuine affection or attraction is unknown as his mother put an immediate stop to the arrangement and Edward capitulated to his forceful mother's opinions. Octavia was said to have been 'devastated' but all the personal views of this period have been edited out (see p. 66). He later became Conservative MP for Northampton in 1895 and never married.

ROBERT BROWNING (7 May 1812–12 December 1889)
The poet met Gertrude and Octavia when they were children. RH Horne, the writer (*Orion*), told him, and Browning himself told Octavia years later, that he had delightedly exclaimed:

'Those are wonderful children; you can talk to them about anything!'

ELIZABETH BARRETT BROWNING (6 March 1806–29 June 1861)
Poet, wife of **Robert Browning** and supporter of Barbara Bodichon's and Octavia Hill's 1856 campaign to change the law of property so that women could retain their personal wealth after marriage via the Married Woman's Property Act (it failed to pass into effective law until 1882). Elizabeth's family had a long history of slave-ownership in Jamaica, and she and Robert had inherited money from slave compensation granted by the government in the wake of abolition for which she had also campaigned. She was rightly concerned by her father's threat to disinherit her if she ever married; he did. **Ruskin** thought her to be the 'the only entirely perfect example of womanhood' despite her long-term ill health and opioid addiction.

EMMA BAUMGARTNER (1830–1911)
Emma was born in Switzerland, corresponded with Octavia Hill and introduced her to her comfortable wealthy family life in Godmanchester, near Cambridge. Emma never married and never had children. She became an ardent financial supporter of the National Trust and is listed as a donor in nearly all the early annual reports. Emma acted as the intimate confidante when Octavia reported her private discussions with **Ruskin**.

> 'We spoke about the wickedness of rich and poor people. Ruskin spoke of little children like angels he saw running about the dirty streets, and thought how they were to be made wicked. I spoke about the frightful want of feeling in all classes; but added that I thought rich people were now waking up to a sense of their duties.'

ROBERT CHALONER (23 September 1776–October 1842)
Robert was awarded slave-owner compensation by the government and was a director in Wentworth, Chaloner and Rishworth, the bank that collapsed and ruined James Hill in 1825. He went bankrupt in 1826. His Yorkshire estate property, however, was saved by his cousin, Earl Fitzwilliam of Wentworth, who appointed him overseer of his 85,000 acre Irish estate at Coolattin where he cleared the land

of its tenant farmers, forcing their emigration from Ireland.

ELLEN CHASE (26 March 1863–September 1949)
Ellen came to London in 1886 from Brookline, Massachusetts, to learn Octavia Hill's techniques of housing management. She produced a book *Tenant Friends in Old Deptford,* based on her time as a volunteer. Octavia wrote the foreword and said,

> 'Her deep human sympathy enabled her to see all that lay below the squalor and violence of the inhabitants, and to realize how much family love redeemed even the most degraded.'

Her relative, Philip Augustus Chase (1834–1903) a banker in Lynn, was on the Massachusetts Board of Trustees for Public Reservations and a member of the Committee for the Preservation of Beautiful and Historical Places in Massachusetts. The work of these bodies was recognised by Frederick Law Olmsted (the landscape architect for New York Central Park and many other notable landmarks) and added to **Robert Hunter**'s ideas for the legal creation of the National Trust. Ellen was a member of the Mayflower Descendants.

JOHN CLARE (13 July 1793–20 May 1864)
A malnourished rural poetry genius from Helpston, Cambridgeshire, who sadly died in a lunatic asylum. He was an impecunious agricultural labourer and, despite a small irregular income from his writings, lived precariously with his wife and children through a period of intensely hurtful common land enclosures and rural dispossession. His painful lament for loss of commons, wild nature and shared freedoms is still agonising to read and very much reflects the impacts of modern intensive agricultural practices. This is a short segment from 'Remembrances':

> Enclosure like a Buonaparte let not a thing remain
> It levelled every bush and tree and levelled every hill
> And hung the moles for traitors
> – though the brook is running still
> It runs a naked brook cold and chill

EMMA CONS (4 March 1838–24 July 1912)
A close teenage friend of Octavia Hill and early pioneering social housing worker as part of Octavia's rent-collecting team from 1864 in Barrett's Court, Oxford Street. She first came into the Hill fold when working as an artist for Caroline Hill when she was managing the Ladies Cooperative Guild, and also later worked for **Ruskin** as a copyist. Her housing fiefdom was mainly in Soho where she was assigned a young **Hardwicke Rawnsley** to train up. In 1879 she grew independent of Octavia (after a row about how to manage the more difficult tenants without evicting them) and started the South London Dwellings Company in Lambeth. She opened a temperance venue in Waterloo called the Royal Victoria Coffee and Music Hall that transformed, with Samuel Morley's money and some Shakespeare and opera, into the Old Vic theatre in 1880. Emma's niece Lilian Baylis managed it and later, Sadlers Wells. Cons, her sister Ellen, and Baylis shared a house at 27 Stockwell Park Road in Lambeth until Emma died. She started the Morley College for female workers at the Old Vic with further donations from Sam Morley and added to the female networks that also managed Lady Margaret Hall Settlement in Kennington. Emma was the weekend partner of Ethel Everest of Chippens Bank, Hever, Kent (where she spent most weekends and where Lilian Baylis scattered her ashes). Ethel was the wealthy third daughter of Sir George Everest, who, despite his vehement objections, had the world's tallest mountain named after him by the Royal Geographical Society. In her will Ethel bequeathed Chippens Bank to the National Trust for use as a rest home in memory of Emma Cons but the Trust refused the bequest. Emma was a tough suffragist and fought her way through the courts to become a London County Councillor, as well as being the first woman to address the Institute of Directors. She was described by Lilian Baylis as

> 'a bit of a tomboy … she always carried a knife and a piece of string in her pocket, even when she was wearing evening dress.'

GEORGIANA COWPER (neé Tollmache, 8 October 1821–1901)
and **WILLIAM COWPER** (Lord Mount Temple, 13 December 1811–
16 October 1888)
Married in 1848 and lived at Broadlands, Romsey, entertaining
a coterie of artists, spiritualists, vegetarians, phrenologists and
homeopaths at their Hampshire estate, including **John Ruskin**.
William was the illegitimate son of Lord Palmerston. His wife
Georgiana had been one of Ruskin's perverse love interests; a
glimpse of her from 50 yards away in Venice apparently gave him an
erection. Annie Andrews, a psychic medium visitor at Broadlands,
told of her ability to have out of body experiences and enter the
realm of the spirits. She announced to a séance there in December
1875 that the recently deceased **Rose La Touche** was with them in
the room standing behind Ruskin. This prompted Ruskin to delve
deeper into the spirit world for the rest of his life.

CHARLES JOHN HUFFAM DICKENS (7 February 1812–9 June 1870)
Acclaimed author, social commentator and the origin of the term
Dickensian. Whilst his father and mother were in Marshalsea Debtors
Prison in Southwark he worked in a rat-infested basement for six
bob a week on Hungerford Stairs sticking labels on boot polish pots.
He never forgot or forgave these harsh lessons of abject poverty
(nor the fact that his mother let him remain there) and the theme
stuck throughout much of his writing, including the name of one of
his fellow child-workers, Bob Fagin. He met Dr Thomas Southwood
Smith whilst living at Tavistock House, Regents Park.

'GEORGE ELIOT' (aka **MARY-ANNE, MARY ANN** or **MARIAN EVANS**)
(22 November 1819–22 December 1880)
Highly influential Victorian author of *Middlemarch*, *Silas Marner* and
The Mill on the Floss. She was a supporter of the Hill sisters' work
and she and her 'husband' George Henry Lewes (a married man with
whom she lived for 20 years) met Caroline Southwood Smith and
her father too. After her own father had declared her too ugly to be
able to marry, Marian became radicalised at the Coventry home of
the Brays who owned the *Coventry Herald and Observer* and who

entertained guests such as **Robert Owen** and Ralph Waldo Emerson. During a trip to Switzerland with the Brays in 1849 she wrote to Sara Henell (although these letters were omitted by her husband when he wrote her biography in 1885, according to research by Pam Johnson in 1989):

> 'I have given you a sad excuse for flirtation, but I have not been beyond seas long enough to make it lawful for you to take a new husband – therefore I come back to you with all a husband's privileges and command you to love me.'

Marian, however, was mainly interested in men. Having come back to London to help edit the *Westminster Review* (to which Thomas Southwood Smith contributed articles) she had a dalliance with the editor John Chapman, who was already living with both his wife and mistress. Obviously the idea of *ménage à trois* seemed worth pursuing as she next lived with philosopher George Henry Lewes, who had an open marriage with Agnes Jervis and a total of seven children by two fathers. The revelation in 1859 that the author of *Adam Bede,* her first acclaimed novel (and Queen Victoria's favourite book at the time), was an adulteress shocked the prudes. It wasn't until the arrival of Queen Victoria's daughter **Princess Louise** at her door in 1877 that she was 'made acceptable'. It was believed by Florence Nightingale that Marian Evans modelled Dorothea Brooke in *Middlemarch* on Octavia Hill. Marian (as she admitted to Harriet Beecher Stowe) modelled Dorothea Brooke's husband, Edward Casaubon, on herself. When she died, as an agnostic humanist, she was not allowed to be buried in Westminster Abbey with the other great writers and poets.

KATE GREENAWAY (17 March 1846 – 6 November 1901)
Kate illustrated Miranda Hill's fairy-story book the *Fairy Spinner* in 1874. Her trend-setting drawings of children's clothing were emulated in real life by Liberty's of London. When she was 36 she came besotted by **John Ruskin** although he was 63. He made himself supervisor of her life and wanted her to send him drawings of her 'girlies' in the nude to feed his perversion. Although she declined

they engaged in Ruskin's peculiar brand of babyish prattle in letters throughout his senility until his death in 1900. She never married and sadly died of breast cancer aged 55.

PRINCESS ALICE OF HESSE-DARMSTADT
(25 April 1843–14 December 1878)
Second daughter of Queen Victoria and champion of many women's causes in Victorian Society. She became a willing patron of the Kyrle Society and despite living much of her short adult life under the shadow of her mother's mourning for Prince Albert, she attempted to conduct herself in ways novel to royal protocols of that era. She visited some of the worst of Octavia's slum properties and was so encouraged by 'the work' that she paid for Octavia's papers to be translated into German and printed so that they might spread amongst towns in her husband's principality where she resided. When the Hessians went to war she arranged hospitals for the wounded and befriended Florence Nightingale so that she could learn more about medicine and nursing treatments. Queen Victoria was perturbed by Alice's interest in gynaecological matters and counselled her younger sister Louise not to let Alice pump her for information about her *'interior'*. Alice had seven children although 'Frittie', when aged three, fell out of a window and died of internal bleeding because of his inherited haemophilia. Her daughter died of diphtheria, which transmitted to the whole household; Alice herself tragically died of the disease in Darmstadt at the young age of 35, a month after her daughter and spookily on the same day as her father. Her last words were 'Dear Papa'.

WILLIAM HODSON (1808–1880)
A radical Owenite acquaintance of James Hill and his brother Thomas, who acted as a partner in the establishment of the 150–200 acre unofficial Owenite Colony at Manea Fen (resident from 1838–41) in the damp Fenland countryside adjacent to the Old Bedford River. There was tension in the camp between locals and those drawn from the industrial cities and between the workers and the shirkers. The colony was a brave attempt to provide an alternative society by

working the land and brick pits and living communally. It produced a newsletter called *The Working Bee*, later with the added sub-title of *Herald of the Hodsonian Community Society* and a motto that clearly indicated a harsher, more biblical understanding of the situation,

'He who will not work neither shall he eat.'

The failure of James Hill's bank caused the ruin of the Colony in 1841 when Hodson was forced to withdraw the funding that kept it all afloat. Manea was also the setting for a strange experiment to prove that the Earth was flat, by Samuel Rowbotham, the self-titled President of the Flat Earth Society. It involved a punt, the Old Bedford River and some very erroneous mathematics.

SIR ROBERT HUNTER (27 October 1844–6 November 1913)
Co-founder of the National Trust and solicitor to the Commons Preservation Society and also solicitor to the General Post Office. His family moved to Dorking when he went to University College London and thereafter came to know the ancient commons of Surrey and the wooded landscapes of the Surrey Hills. He entered, but did not win the first prize, in a £400 competition offered by Sir Henry Peek on 'The Preservation of Commons in the Neighbourhood of the Metropolis'. Robert's essay expounded the view that such urban fringe commons should not be enclosed because they provided 'health, comfort and convenience' for the nearby inhabitants. His law firm of Fawcett, Horne and Hunter became solicitors for the Commons Preservation Society and won monumental legal battles to save Hampstead Heath, Wimbledon, Tooting, Plumstead, and Berkhamsted Commons. He later joined forces with the City of London to save Epping Forest, opened by Queen Victoria in 1882, making it 'available for her people's enjoyment'. He chaired the Kyrle Society's Open Spaces sub-committee and helped pave the pathways that led to the formation of the National Trust. He received a knighthood in 1894.

JAMIESON B. HURRY (1857–1930)

The son-in-law of Arthur Hill. He and his wife donated the money to buy the land for the Arthur Hill Memorial Baths at Cemetery Junction in Reading. He also bought land at One Tree Hill, Kent, as a memorial to Arthur and donated it to the National Trust. Jamieson was a respected local doctor and in his spare time wrote books on such diverse subjects as the dye-plant woad, the rise and fall of Reading Abbey, Egyptian pharaonic medicine and Imhotep, the poverty cycle and nursing administration. In his obituary in the British Medical Journal he was quoted as saying that it is

'a rich man's duty to give to the poor'.

SOPHIA JEX-BLAKE (21 January 1840–7 January 1912)

According to her diaries, Sophia Jex-Blake was deeply attracted to Octavia Hill and they shared at least one passionate kiss. Her diary for 17 May 1860 records the conversation with Octavia ahead of a trip to Wales and ends with the line

'She sunk her head on my lap silently, raised it in tears, and then such a kiss'.

Sophia met Octavia at Queen's College when she was 18 and Octavia 20. Seemingly she set about seducing Octavia and moved into the Hill home for nine months before being expelled by Caroline Hill. In August 1860 Octavia wrote to Sophia:

'London feels strangely desolate, the lamps looked as they used to look, pityless and unending as I walked home last night, and knew I could not go to you … I look forward to bright long days in which I shall learn more about you, and watch with unending and unfathomable love and sympathy your upward growth, and we may look back together on our lives, as I often do on my own'.

There are also suggestions in her diaries that Sophia had 'an affection' for Miranda Hill, whom she called by a pet name 'Frid' – an affection that seems to have been stimulated by Miranda. In Sophia's diary entry for 31 December 1861 she provides a sad retrospective on that tumultuous year.

'The opening of the year, bright, clear, hopeful ... Our delight in our new house – its quiet and peace ... No bar to happiness ... Then the return of Frid and Florence. My unwilling acquaintance ripening gradually into love for Frid, called forth perhaps first by her great love for me. Then our glorious Whitsuntide at Hurst – Octa and I. The few days (Thursday to Tuesday) pure unmixed heart sunshine. Purer and deeper if possible than that of Wales. Then the strange double summons on May 21st. Together to London. The hurried tea, the night mail, the parting hand pressure as the train moved, 'in the sure and certain hope' – is it blasphemous so to use such words? I think not. There was a glorious churchlike solemnity always on our love. Well – then the five months parting – hard it seemed then but painless – heaven – to what came after. Never seemed our love truer, deeper, purer – I know though *now* that mine *could* be all three'.

Following her expulsion from the Hill's Nottingham Place home, Sophia went to Edinburgh to enrol at the University to undertake a course in medicine despite the fact that women were barred from study by the University authorities. She stuck at it to become one of the 'Edinburgh Seven' female medical students, the cause of the Surgeons' Hall Riots in Edinburgh in 1870 (when a 200-strong gang of misogynist thugs tried to prevent them from attending exams) and the first practising female doctor in Scotland. Sophia never forgot Octavia and, despite living most of the rest of her life with Margaret Read, made over all her worldly goods to Octavia in a series of wills. Dr Margaret Read, companion, lover and biographer of Sophia Jex-Blake, famously invented the scientific term 'isotope' but was denied recognition of her work (and a Nobel Prize) because she was a woman.

JOHN KYRLE (1637–1724)

The poet Alexander Pope was responsible for enhancing the reputation of John Kyrle (or Kirle) in his poem 'The Uses of Riches'. Kyrle was wealthy enough not to work, the son of the MP for Leominster, barrister, cyderist and unmarried man looked after by a relative, Miss Judith Bubb. Pope alleged that he was the instigator of multiple, marvellous, social amenity and building improvements in the town of Ross-on-Wye, Herefordshire, and gave him the title 'the Man of Ross'. Some of this was undoubtedly fake news, some based on real events, but by most accounts John Kyrle was a meritorious, mellow fellow who drank local cider, smoked a pipe or two, arbitrated in local disputes before they reached the expense of going to law and probably used his and others' money philanthropically to make life better for residents. Pope, who hovered around the rich and famous of his era, saw that most of their excessive wealth was spent selfishly and wanted to depict a character with heroic selflessness as a contrast that would make society sit up and take notice. Samuel Taylor Coleridge followed suit, writing lines to Kyrle's memory on a Wye walking tour whilst trying to forget Mary Evans. When, eventually, the daughter of Queen Victoria was installed as Patron of a society named in his honour, the myth of John Kyrle became reality, or as Dr Johnson said of Pope,

> 'Wonders are willingly told and willingly heard.'

ROSE LA TOUCHE (3 January 1848–25 May 1875)

The subject of **John Ruskin**'s greatest infatuation had been introduced to Ruskin by her wealthy parents who wanted the social prestige of him as her art tutor. She was nine and he was 38. Ruskin's marriage proposal around her eighteenth birthday in 1867 shocked her parents so much that they contacted Effie Millais to understand more about Ruskin's bearing as a husband. Effie suggested that he was 'utterly incapable of making a woman happy' and that

> 'he is quite unnatural ... and his conduct to me was impure in the highest degree.'

Ruskin, however, had already planned out their matrimonial future in a cottage provided by his Guild of St George in the grounds of Broadlands near Romsey in Hampshire, and their life around the Cowpers and like-minded utopian escapees from industrialism. However, Rose dumped him and Ruskin went into a downward spiral. It worsened after her death, on 25 May 1875 in Dublin, probably from *anorexia nervosa* when she was just 27. The artist made an extraordinary drawing of Rose on her deathbed that January. It is thought that Nabokov's novel *Lolita* was based on this relationship. Ruskin's depression over her death probably fed his attack on Octavia Hill.

HENRY MAYHEW (25 November 1812–25 July 1887)
Co-founder of *Punch* and author of critically influential books on the lives of the Victorian underclasses. In particular the book *London Labour and the London Poor* was handed to Octavia to read by a fellow worker at the Ladies Cooperative Guild when she had just arrived (aged 13) to begin work at Russell Place, Fitzroy Square with her mother and sisters. The culture shock was transformative. Before descending into the grim and ghastly poverty of Victorian London described in detail by Mayhew, the girls had been part of the 'distressed gentle-folk' but funded adequately by their middle-class grandfather. The shock made an impact that never left the sisters and was to drive their choices until death.

FREDERICK DENISON 'F D' MAURICE (29 August 1805–1 April 1872)
Radical preacher and leading member of the Christian Socialists. He employed Octavia as an overseer of the Ragged School 'toy-workers' at the Ladies Cooperative Guild, where she also became an avid fan of his sermons combining Christianity with social welfare issues. Like **Ruskin**, F D Maurice rejected competition as being fundamentally unchristian and preferred cooperation as the way of the Christian Brotherhood. He started Working Men's Associations, the Working Men's College and a number of cooperatives. From 1848 to 1854 he led the Christian Socialists. He was denounced by fellow religious folk for some minor theological differences but was considered by

Charles Kingsley (author of *The Water Babies*, *Hereward the Wake* and *Westward Ho!)* to be

> 'the most beautiful human soul whom God has ever allowed me to meet with'.

CHARLES EDMUND MAURICE (1843 – 4 February 1927)

Son of Rev. **FD Maurice**; married Emily Hill in 1872. Author of *Life of Octavia Hill as told in her letters*, published in 1913 shortly after her death, and a number of other books including *The Revolutionary Movement of 1848–9 in Italy, Austria-Hungary and Germany* and *Lives of English Popular Leaders*.

WILLIAM MORRIS (24 March 1834 – 3 October 1896)

Socialist revolutionary, poet, artist, craft designer, polymath and anti-industrialist. Highly influenced by **Ruskin** and Carlyle, he became the leader of the Arts and Crafts Movement and sponsor of the Pre-Raphaelite Brotherhood, as well as author of *News from Nowhere*. He was brought up in comfortable surroundings in a large country house in Essex and was well educated although he hated boarding school. His father made money from stocks and shares until his early death in 1847. The Morris family had to downsize from a country mansion to a smaller but hardly less well-appointed house. Morris inherited wealth from his father who was a shareholder and director of the Great Devon Consolidated Mines (Great Consols). Morris and his brother then became shareholders and made money when the mines became the most successful copper mine in the world in 1864, producing £300,000 profit after all expenses from 90,000 tons of high-grade copper ore. When the copper ran out it became the biggest arsenic producer in the world, for a time, exporting both ore and arsenic through Morwellham Quay (near the National Trust's Cotehele Estate). The mine was under investigation for its working practices when it began to wane. It's possible that the campaigning work of Thomas Southwood Smith to prevent children working in West Country mines impacted upon Great Consols. Morris spoke warmly about the Kyrle Society

'I feel there is a difficulty in the way of my advocating before you the claims of the Kyrle Society to public support; its case is almost too good to bear talking about it'.

The Kyrle Society's enemies he said were 'Carelessness, Ugliness and Squalor'.

'For it is idle to talk about popularizing art, if you are not prepared to popularize reverence for nature also, both among the poor and the rich'.

ROBERT OWEN (14 May 1771–17 November 1858)
Pioneering industrialist with a social conscience who sought to improve the living conditions of those working for his enterprises at New Lanark Mills, Scotland, which became the most profitable cotton mill in Europe. Owen's mills and workers' housing scheme became a celebrated model of benign capitalism with many dissenters attracted to the methods and ideas deployed by him. These followers became known as 'Owenites' and took this philosophy to other places where they invested in or fantasised about Owenite Colonies. Owen provided good housing, schools and open spaces for his workforce. It was a scheme not replicated anywhere else at the time. Owen thought he could create a worldview 'free of envy, competition and vice' based on mutuality and goodness, and campaigned for a 'New Moral World'. He visited the Hill's Wisbech School in person and corresponded with Caroline Hill at the Ladies Cooperative Guild. The Cooperative Movement aspects of Utopian Socialism and his later belief in Spiritualism form his legacy.

JOHANN HEINRICH PESTALOZZI
(12 January 1746–17 February 1827)
Swiss educationalist, whose beliefs in children's individualism over industrial teaching by rote were contrary to the methods of the time but paved the way for the modern education systems of much of the Western world. Pestalozzi based his system on equalising the educational importance of skills of hand, heart and head (doing,

believing and thinking). In recent years in Britain, concepts such as 'Forest Schools' and 'learning outdoors' or 'learning outside the classroom' have had limited success in challenging the mainstream indoor educational chicken coops. Pestalozzi's thinking is at the centre of the Hill story, because without Caroline Hill's unbending belief in the rightness of his approach to experiential learning in nature, promotion of doing good things and moral education, as well as practical applications of hand and mind, the gifts of this thinking would not have been passed on. Everything the Hill children, under Caroline's close instruction, managed to achieve in life can in some way be traced back to Pestalozzi. As a child in Switzerland, Johann Pestalozzi accompanied his grandfather, a man of religion, on his tours of the poor in both rural and industrial places. As with Octavia Hill's later experiences in London the shock of such extreme poverty on young Pestalozzi had a deep impact. He resolved to build a school (Neuhof) where peasant children could not only learn a skilled trade and so learn to escape poverty as adults but also pay their way in early years education by hand-making small-scale textile products to sell. The Neuhof School couldn't match the industrial competition and failed, but it taught Pestalozzi to refine his thinking. Caroline Hill would have passed these ideas on to her children and they can be seen in the experiences of the Ragged School toy-makers and Octavia's rigorous book-keeping, desperate to make it pay, which surely came from this Swiss source. Similarly, her drive to take poor urban children and adults away from the dark inner-city grime to green fields and sunlight was a direct Pestalozzian influence.

SAMUEL PLIMSOLL (10 February 1824 – 3 June 1898)
MP for Liverpool and initiator of the ship load-measuring line, who later gave his name to the canvas and rubber-soled shoe invented by the Liverpool Rubber Company in the 1830s. An unlikely freedom fighter, he took part in the first 'mass trespass' in the Lake District. His social conscience to help the downtrodden (sorry) had been stirred by personally suffering destitution in London.

CANON HARDWICKE DRUMMOND RAWNSLEY
(29 September 1851–28 May 1920)

Co-founder of the National Trust and responsible for providing an early preservationist focus in the Ruskin-associated landscapes and scenic viewpoints of the Lake District. **Ruskin** and **Rawnsley** met frequently at Brantwood, Ruskin's house on Lake Coniston. He was trained by **Emma Cons** as a housing worker in London but, for some undiscovered reason, left London's Soho and was given a position at Wray deep in the rural Lake District. Here he married local lass Edith Fletcher from Ambleside, met the wealthy Potter family who had rented Wray Castle for their summer vacations and was introduced to 16-year-old Beatrix Potter (Rawnsley was then 31). Rawnsley encouraged Beatrix to publish her illustrated stories and helped make literary history when Peter Rabbit appeared in 1902. Rupert Potter later became the first ever life member of the National Trust and his daughter Beatrix donated most of her estate, 15 Herdwick sheep farms and £4000 to the National Trust when she died. The Trust's central office is called 'Heelis' after her married name. Octavia put him off accepting the post of Bishop of Madagascar in 1898 to focus on preserving the Lake District. It is believed that this offer might have been a bit of Establishment skullduggery to get rid of him as an objector to various industrial investments. Rawnsley was born in Shiplake near Henley-on-Thames in 1851 and had the great Victorian hero and Arctic explorer Sir John Franklin as an uncle. His father was Vicar of Shiplake and had officiated at his friend Tennyson's wedding. At Balliol College Oxford, Hardwicke met **Ruskin** and became part of the Hinksey Road Gang. In the Lake District Rawnsley took children to visit nature much as Octavia did and became the President of the Cumberland Nature Club. In line with many new thinkers he developed many fringe ideas; strong pro-views on organic farming, brown bread, mountain-top bonfires and film censorship; and strong contra-views on water pollution, slot machines and saucy seaside postcards.

JOHN RUSKIN (8 February 1819–20 January 1900)

The reach, complexity and impact of John Ruskin's life are hard to express with brevity. Much of his thinking still informs modern ideas and institutional processes. He was a polymath who, at a young age, had his mother read him every word in the Bible and then immediately read it again. He later inherited a huge £200,000 fortune (from his father's wine business, now Allied-Domecq) lived with his widowed mother in South London and became the Victorian era's most influential art critic and man of letters. His pushy parents wanted him to be educated to become either the Archbishop of Canterbury or the Poet Laureate but also facilitated extensive travel to the many vineyard areas of Europe where the clever, observant young boy witnessed both the immense beauty of the Alps but also the grinding poverty of the Swiss peasants (much in the way that **Pestalozzi** had). These contrasts found their way into his thoughts on art, social organisation and inequalities, work and craftsmanship. He defined 'the truth of natural beauty' in art by encouraging his followers to go out and study geology, meteorology, plants and all the forms of nature. The Oxford Museum of Natural History is a product of his encouragement of natural science education. Ruskin was awarded the Professorship of the Slade School of Fine Art at Oxford in 1869, despite getting a pass degree, and mingled with Charles Dodgson, George MacDonald, Oscar Wilde and **Hardwicke Rawnsley** either as colleagues or pupils. He was heavily influenced by the thoughts of Thomas Carlyle. He was the keeper of the torch for JMW Turner's artistic work, although the idea (put about by Ruskin himself) that he may have torched the pornographic sketches among JMW's 30,000 artworks seems to be an 1858 subterfuge to avoid difficulties with the newly passed Obscene Publications Act 1857.

He rejected 'art for art's sake' by libelling Whistler. Ruskin's enormous contemporary influence over the wealthy and aspirational created trends and gave focus to many land and art acquisitions by the early preservationists. He was an overseer of the rise of the

Pre-Raphaelite Brotherhood that painted the beautiful, mainly female, icons of heroic acts, despairing self-sacrifice and pseudo-medieval fantasies. He claimed to stand for the craftsmanship of the working man and established the Guild of St George to further this utopian concept, and was prepared to fund various social experiments such as those proposed by Octavia Hill. However, he was also driven by sexual perversions for young girls that still defy accurate categorisation; possibilities include nympholepsy or autoerotic paedophilia as some writers have suggested. Thus his influential views on beauty and untouched virginal landscapes and his hatred of industrial despoliation, that made his opinions stand out in a society of wanton industrialists, may have been connected to both his childhood love of nature and to his adult sexuality. Nobody knows what's true. However, in May 1886 Ruskin wrote to his doctor:

> 'I like my girls from ten to sixteen – allowing of 17 or 18 as long as they're not in love with anybody but me – I've got some darlings of 8, 12, 14 just now …'

Ruskin 'married' the beautiful teenage Euphemia (Effie) Chalmers Gray in Cumbria on 10 April 1848 but never consummated the marriage. Ruskin's pursuit of Effie started when she was just ten. When she was twelve in 1841 he wrote the fantasy story *King of the Golden River* for her. After the marriage annulment in 1854 Ruskin never 'married' again but was infatuated with a number of young girls, including **Rose La Touche**. After Rose's death he became deeply involved with spiritualism and at a séance at the Cowper's house believed he had been instructed by the 'spirit' of Rose to marry another young girl, Tenny Watson.

JOHN GEORGE SHAW-LEFEVRE (12 June 1831–19 April 1928)
Chairman of the Commons Preservation Society, Britain's oldest conservation body founded in 1865. Later, as Lord Eversley, he became President. In his 1912 book of the history of the Open Spaces Movement, *Commons, Forests and Footpaths*, he mentions Octavia Hill just four times and refers to her merely as sitting on various

committees. It seems that there was something amiss between them that may have been partially responsible for the ten-year delay in setting up the National Trust. It is possible that he wanted the focus to remain legislative and about commons, footpaths and open spaces rather than acquiring possession. It is possible that he was just miffed. **Robert Hunter** and Edward North Buxton co-wrote the introduction to the book and add a hint by stating:

> 'the simple idea that led to the battle over the London commons – that large towns required Open Spaces – has developed in many and varied directions ... the recreation of crowded populations led to Parks and Gardens. Gardens out of disused churchyards ... the movement for the provision of Playing Fields ... the preservation of beautiful views ... and the formation of Garden Cities and Suburbs.'

They continued:

> 'It may be doubted whether the Kyrle Society ... or the Metropolitan Public Gardens Association or the National Trust would have come into existence so soon or in quite the same way had not the Commons Preservation Society insisted on the necessity of Open Spaces to secure the health of towns and the reasonable enjoyment of life by those who live in towns'.

SAMUEL SMILES (23 December 1812–16 April 1904)
Samuel lived in Leeds and most likely met James and Caroline Hill there. Smiles took a role in the Leeds branch of the Chartist movement in 1840 seeking after the things that we now take for granted as part of the Parliamentary process, such as secret ballots and equal-sized voting districts. As rage grew when these simple requests were denied the Chartists became more militant but all involved agreed that

> 'mere political reform will not cure the manifold evils which now afflict society'.

In 1859 Samuel Smiles, concerned by rising violence, wrote the book *Self-Help* that was highly influential in considering how the poor and unrepresented might best elevate themselves and was applied by Octavia Hill in her dealings with her tenants. Smiles is also the great-great-grandfather of Bear Grylls, Chief Scout and TV adventurer.

HARRIOT YORKE (1843 – 31 October 1930)

A wealthy woman of independent means from an old family. Her father, the Rev. Charles Isaac Yorke, was the vicar of Shenfield, Essex. The family was descended from the Yorkes of Hardwicke, Gloucestershire. She and Octavia Hill lived together in a cottage in Kent called 'Larksfield' as well as in London for over 30 years. Harriot's wealth provided the money for many of Octavia's continental holidays, scenic tours of Britain and therapeutic spa treatments. Harriot took on a number of Octavia's duties in the National Trust after her death. She died aged 87 on 31 October 1930 and, as planned in advance with Octavia's solicitors, was buried in Miranda's and Octavia's shared grave at Crockham churchyard. She called Octavia 'her lion' and Octavia called her 'The Keeper'.

Further reading

Anon (1891) Kyrle Society Annual Report

Baigent, Elizabeth and Cowell, Ben (eds) (2016), *Nobler Imaginings and Mightier Struggles. Octavia Hill, social activism and the remaking of British society*, Institute of Historical Research

Bailey, Catherine (2008), *Black Diamonds: The Rise and Fall of an English Dynasty*, Penguin.

Birch, Jules (2012), *The Victorian values of Octavia Hill*, www.julesbirch.com

Brittain, Marcus (2017), *Ouse Washes Archaeology: Manea Colony Investigation*, Cambridge Archaeology Unit.

Burnett, J (1978), *A Social History of Housing 1815-1970*, David & Charles

* Darley, Gillian (1990), *Octavia Hill: A Life*, Constable.

* Darley, Gillian (2010), *Octavia Hill: Social Reformer and Founder of the National Trust*, Francis Boutle

Digby, Anne and Stewart, John (1996), *Gender, Health and Welfare*, Routledge

* Eversley, Lord (1910), *Commons, Forests and Footpaths*, Cassell & Co

Fedden, Robin (1974), *The National Trust Past and Present*, Jonathan Cape

Gaze, John (1988), *Figures in a Landscape: A History of the National Trust*, Barrie & Jenkins

Helm, Dieter (2015) *Natural Capital: Valuing the Planet*, Yale

* Hill, Octavia (1875, reprinted), *Homes of the London Poor*, Dodo Press

* Hill, William Thompson (1956), *Octavia Hill: Pioneer of the National Trust and Housing Reformer*, Hutchison

Hoare, Phillip (2005), *England's Lost Eden*, Fourth Estate

* Hunter, Robert (1884), *A Suggestion for the Better Preservation of Open Spaces*, Commons Preservation Society

Jones, S, ed (2012), *The Enduring Relevance of Octavia Hill*, available at http://www.demos.co.uk/publications/octaviahill

Lesbian History Group (1989), *Not a Passing Phase: Reclaiming Lesbians in History 1840-1985*, Women's Press

* Lewes, Gertrude (1898), *Dr Southwood Smith: a retrospect*, Blackwood

Louv, Richard (2010), *Last Child in the Woods*, Atlantic Books

Marsh, Jan (1982), *Back to the Land: The Pastoral Impulse in England, from 1880 to 1914*, Quartet

Mayhew, Henry (1861), *London Labour and the London Poor*, Griffin Bohn

* Maurice, Charles Edmund (1913), *Life of Octavia Hill as told in her letters*, Macmillan

* Moberley Bell, Enid (1942), *Octavia Hill: A Biography*, Constable

Octavia Foundation (various) (2015), *A Life More Noble: Reflections on Octavia Hill's Ambition of Nobility for All*, Octavia

Olwig, Kenneth Robert (2002), *Landscape, Nature and the Body Politic: From Britain's Renaissance to America's New World*, University of Wisconsin Press

Ouvry, Elinor Southwood (1933), *Octavia Hill: Letters to Fellow Workers 1864–1911*, Adelphi Books

Preston, Rebecca (2003), *An Extended History of Myatt's Field Park*

Reynolds, Fiona (2016), *The Fight for Beauty*, Oneworld

Rodgers, Christopher and Mackay, Duncan (2017), *Creating new commons for the twenty-first century: innovative legal models for green space, Journal of Environmental Planning and Management* available at http://www.tandfonline.com/doi/full/10.1080/09640568.2017.1333407

* Todd, Margaret Georgina (1918), *The Life of Sophia Jex-Blake 1859–1918*, Macmillan

Vaughan, Philip (2011), *A Centenary Memoir on the Arthur Hill Memorial Baths*

Weideger, Paula (1994), *Gilding the Acorn: Behind the facade of the National Trust,* Simon and Schuster

Whelan, Robert (2005), *Octavia Hill's Letters to Fellow Workers*, Kyrle Books

Whelan, R, ed (1998), *Octavia Hill and the Social Housing Debate*, available at http://www.civitas.org.uk/pdf/rr3.pdf

Williams, WH. (1965), *A Short History of the Society and its work 1865–1965*, Commons, Open Spaces and Footpaths Preservation Society

* https://historicengland.org.uk/research/inclusive-heritage/ lgbtq-heritage-project/workplaces-and-creativity/ independent-women/

http://www.independent.co.uk/news/uk/home-news/britains- colonial-shame-slave-owners-given-huge-payouts-after- abolition-8508358.html

http://www.herstoria.com/octavia-hill-1838-1912

http://www.historytoday.com/richard-cavendish/ death-kate-greenaway

http://www.encyclopedia.com/children/ academic-and-educational-journals/greenaway-kate-1846-1901

https://en.wikisource.org/wiki/ Life_of_Octavia_Hill_as_told_in_her_letters/Chapter_11

* http://winsomegriffin.com/Newsham/Isaac_Jecks.html (family research by Murray Jecks-Johnston and John Barnett)

http://www.stpaulsbrookline.org

http://www.octaviahousing.org.uk

http://www.octaviafoundation.org.uk

* http://www.octaviahill.org

http://www.ousewashes.org.uk

http://www.independent.co.uk/life-style/rawnsley-thou-shouldst-be-living-at-this-hour-1610966.html

https://www.lostlidos.co.uk/2016/10/24/arthur-hill-memorial-baths-reading

http://www2.readingmuseum.org.uk/collections/social-history/britain-bayeux-tapestry/

http://www.infed.org/archives/communitydevelopment/octavia_hill_space_for_the_people.htm

https://www.theguardian.com/artanddesign/2005/feb/12/art.art

* https://www.nationaltrust.org.uk/features/octavia-hill-her-life-and-legacy

https://en.wikipedia.org/wiki/Grenfell_Tower_fire

http://infed.org/mobi/johann-heinrich-pestalozzi-pedagogy-education-and-social-justice/

https://www.gov.uk/government/collections/monitor-of-engagement-with-the-natural-environment-survey-purpose-and-results

http://www.dieterhelm.co.uk/assets/secure/documents/Green-Belt-Paper-.pdf

https://www.gov.uk/government/groups/natural-capital-committee

http://journals.sagepub.com/doi/abs/10.1177/0013916582141001

http://www.scenicsolutions.com.au/Theory.html

Two Rivers Press has been publishing in and
about Reading since 1994. Founded by the artist
Peter Hay (1951–2003), the press continues to delight
readers, local and further afield, with its varied list
of individually designed, thought-provoking books.